D1649592
Polish
phrasebook

Consultant
Hania Forss

First published 2007

Reprint 10 9 8 7 6 5 4 3 2 1 0
Typeset by Davidson Pre-Press, Glasgow
Printed in Malaysia by Imago

www.collins.co.uk

ISBN 13 978-0-00-724682-3
ISBN 10 0-00-724682-X

Using your phrasebook

Your *Collins Gem Phrasebook* is designed to help you locate the exact phrase you need, when you need it, whether on holiday or for business. If you want to adapt the phrases, you can easily see where to substitute your own words using the dictionary section, and the clear, full-colour layout gives you direct access to the different topics.

The Gem Phrasebook includes:

- Over 70 topics arranged thematically. Each phrase is accompanied by a simple pronunciation guide which eliminates any problems pronouncing foreign words.

- A top ten tips section to safeguard against any cultural faux pas, giving essential dos and don'ts for situations involving local customs or etiquette.

- Practical hints to make your stay trouble free, showing you where to go and what to do when dealing with everyday matters such as travel or hotels and offering valuable tourist information.

- Face to face sections so that you understand

what is being said to you. These example mini-dialogues give you a good idea of what to expect from a real conversation.

- Common announcements and messages you may hear, ensuring that you never miss the important information you need to know when out and about.

- A clearly laid-out 3000-word dictionary means you will never be stuck for words.

- A basic grammar section which will enable you to build on your phrases.

- A list of public holidays to avoid being caught out by unexpected opening and closing hours, and to make sure you don't miss the celebrations!

It's worth spending time before you embark on your travels just looking through the topics to see what is covered and becoming familiar with what might be said to you.

Whatever the situation, your *Gem Phrasebook* is sure to help!

Contents

Pronouncing Polish

Spelling and pronouncing Polish are not difficult once you know a few basic rules. This book has been designed so that as you read the pronunciation of the phrases, you can follow the Polish too. This will help you recognize how Polish is pronounced and give you a feeling for the rhythm of the language. Here are five simple rules to follow:

1 Some letters are marked with additional signs above or below them to indicate different pronunciation: ą, ę, ć, ł, ń, ó, ś, ź and ż. Examples:

Polish	sounds like	example pronunciation
ą	on **sąd**	**sond** (in the middle of the word)
	ow **są**	**sow** (at the end of the word)
ę	en **ręka**	**renka** (in the middle of the word)
	e **będę**	**bende** (at the end of the word)

Polish	sounds like		example pronunciation
ć/cz/ci			(similar pronunciation)
	ch	ćma	chma
		czek	chek
		ciemno	chemno
ł	w	ładne	wadne
ń/ni	n y	niebo	n yebo
ó (= u)	oo	bóg	book
ś/si	sh	śmiech	shmieh
ź/ż/zi			(similar pronunciation)
	zh	żona	zhona
		zima	zheema
		źle	zhle

2 These consonants are pronounced differently in Polish than they are in English:

Polish	sounds like		example pronunciation
c	ts	cena	tsena
ch = h	h	chałwa	hawva
j	y	jestem	yestem
r (strong)	r	rower	rover
w	v	wino	veeno

3 The consonants below are represented by two letters, but make just one sound:

Polish	sounds like	example pronunciation
cz	ch **czek**	chek
sz	sh **szal**	shal
rz	zh **rzeka**	zheka
dz	dz **dzwon**	dzvon
dź	dj **dźwig**	djveek
dż	dj **dżem**	djem

4 The above consonants may appear in groups which don't exist in English, but are very typical in Polish, for example:

Polish	sounds like	example pronunciation
szcz	shch **Szczecin**	shchecheen
prz	psh **przepraszam**	psheprasham
ść	shch **cześć**	cheshch
trz	tsh **trzy**	tshi

5 The remaining consonants: **b**, **d**, **g**, **h**, **k**, **l**, **m**, **n**, **p**, **s**, **t**, **z** are pronounced almost as in English. However, at the end of a word or when together with certain voiceless consonants, the pronunciation of some voiced consonants changes into their voiceless counterparts, for example b, d, g, w, z, ż and rz change into **p**, **t**, **k**, **f**, **s**, and **sh** (for both ż and rz), respectively.

Spelling	**Pronunciation**
klub	kloop
ślad	shlat
bóg	book
kwiat	kf yat
wóz	voos
też	tesh
lekarz	lekash

Stress usually falls on the second-to-last syllable. We have indicated the stressed syllable by using **bold** in the pronunciation of the words.

Top ten tips

1 The percentage of alcohol allowed while driving is nil.

2 The most common toast is **na zdrowie** (to your health). Sometimes, '**sto lat**' is said, which means 100 years, with the hope that you will live to be 100 years old.

3 You might need to remove your shoes before entering a Polish home. If you see shoes lined up at the entrance, it means you are requested to remove yours as well.

4 Poland is a very religious country so remember to cover your shoulders and legs when visiting religious buildings.

5 Names are attached to particular days of the year. For example, if you are called Lech you will celebrate your name day on 12 August. Name day celebrations are as important as birthdays!

6 Dinner on Christmas Eve (**Wigilia**) consists of 12 courses.

7 There are four main meals in Poland: breakfast (**pierwsze sniadanie**), second breakfast (**drugie sniadanie**) at around 11 am, the main meal of the day at 4 pm, and supper between 8 and 9 pm.

8 Use **Pan** and **Pani** (Mr and Mrs) before people's names.

9 Many older Poles still kiss a lady's hand to show good manners.

10 Side lights in cars must be switched on from dusk till dawn, and at all times from 1 October to the end of February.

Talking to people

Hello/goodbye, yes/no

Polish people can be quite formal in their greeting. If you don't know someone well, the best greeting to use is **dzień dobry** (literally good day). This is what you should use if you are unsure how formal to be. **Cześć** is used among family and friends.

Please	**Proszę** **pro**-she
Thank you (very much)	**Dziękuję (bardzo)** djen-**koo**-ye (**bar**-dzo)
You're welcome!	**Proszę (bardzo)!** **pro**-she **bar**-dzo!
Yes	**Tak** tak
No	**Nie** n ye
Yes, please	**Tak, proszę** tak, **pro**-she

No, thanks	**Nie, dziękuję** n ye, djen-**koo**-ye
OK!	**Dobrze!** **do**-**b**zhe!
Sir/Mr...	**Pan...** pan...
Madam/Mrs...	**Pani...** **pa**-nee...
Hello	**Dzień dobry/Cześć** djen **do**-bry/cheschch
Goodbye	**Do widzenia** do vee-**dze**-nya
Hi/Bye	**Cześć** cheshch
See you later	**Do zobaczenia!** do zo-ba-**che**-nya!
Good evening	**Dobry wieczór** **do**-bri **vye**-choor
Good night	**Dobranoc** do-**bra**-nots
See you tomorrow	**Do jutra** do **yoo**-tra
Excuse me!/Sorry!	**Przepraszam/Przykro mi!** pshe-**pra**-sham/**pshi**-kro mee!
Excuse me! (to get past in a crowd)	**Przepraszam** pshe-**pra**-sham

I don't understand	**Nie rozumiem** nye ro-**zoo**-myem
I don't speak Polish	**Nie mówię po polsku** nye **moo**-vye po **pol**-skoo

Key phrases

Do you have...?	**Czy jest...?** chi yest...?
Do you have a timetable?	**Czy jest rozkład jazdy?** chi yest **ros**-kwat **yaz**-di?
Do you have a room?	**Czy jest wolny pokój?** chi yest **vol**-ni **po**-kooy?
Do you have any milk?	**Czy jest mleko?** chi yest **mle**-ko?
I'd like...	**P(op)roszę (o)...** **p(op)ro**-she (o)...
We'd like... (in a restaurant)	**P(op)rosimy (o)...** p(op)ro-**shee**-mi (o)...
I'd like an ice-cream	**P(op)roszę (o) lody** **p(op)ro**-she (o) **lo**-di
We'd like some salad, please	**P(op)rosimy (o) sałatkę** p(op)ro-**shee**-mi (o) sa-**wat**-ke

Another espresso	**Jeszcze jedną kawę**
	yesh-che **yed**-now **ka**-ve
Another beer	**Jeszcze jedno piwo**
	yesh-che **yed**-no p**ee**-vo
Some more water	**Jeszcze raz wodę**
	yesh-che **raz vo**-de
How much...?	**Ile...?**
	ee-le...?
How much does it cost?	**Ile to kosztuje?**
	ee-le to kosh-**too**-ye?
Where is...?	**Gdzie jest...?**
	gdje yest...?
Where are...?	**Gdzie są...?**
	gdje sow...?
How to get to...? (on foot)	**Jak dojść do...?**
	yak doyshch do...?
the museum	**muzeum**
	moo-ze-oom
the station	**stacji**
	sta-tsyee
How to get to...? (by transport)	**Jak dojechać do...?**
	yak do-**ye**-hach do...?
Warsaw	**Warszawy**
	var-**sha**-vi
There is...	**Jest...**
	yest...

There are...	**Są...**
	sow...
There isn't...	**Nie ma...**
	nye ma...
There aren't any...	**Nie ma...**
	nye ma...
When?	**Kiedy?**
	kye-di?
At what time?	**O której godzinie?**
	o **ktoo**-rey go-**djee**-nye?
today	**dzisiaj**
	djee-shay
tomorrow	**jutro**
	yoot-ro
Can I?	**Czy można...?**
	chi **mozh**-na...?
smoke	**palić**
	pa-leech
taste it	**to spróbować**
	to sproo-**bo**-vach
How does this work?	**Jak to działa?**
	yak to **dja**-wa?
What does this mean?	**Co to znaczy?**
	tso to **zna**-chi?

Key phrases

Signs and notices

Ciągnąć	pull
Damska	ladies toilet
Dla niepalących	for non-smokers
Dla palących	for smokers
Do wynajęcia	to let
Dworzec kolejowy/ autobusowy	railway/bus station
Godziny urzędowania	office hours
Godziny zwiedzania	visiting hours
Instrukcja obsługi	instructions for use
Kasa	ticket office *or* cashier
Komisariat policji	police station
Kościół	church
Lotnisko/port lotniczy	airport
Męska	men's toilet
Niebezpieczeństwo	danger
Nieczynne	closed
Nie działa	out of order
Nie blokować wjazdu/wejścia	do not obstruct entrance
Nie dotykać	do not touch
Odjazdy	departures (trains, buses)
Odloty	departures (flights)

Okazje	bargains
Opóźnienie	delay
Ostrożnie	careful
Otwarte	open
Parking	car park
Parter	ground floor
Piętro	floor (storey)
Pchać	push
Poczekalnia	waiting room
Poczta	post office/mail
Postój taksówek	taxi stand
Przyjazdy	arrivals (trains and buses)
Przyloty	arrivals (flights)
Przystanek autobusowy	bus stop
Spożyć przed...	use by/best before...
Stacja metra	metro station
Szkoła	school
Szpital	hospital
Uwaga	attention/caution
Wejście	entrance (on foot)
Winda	lift
Wjazd	entrance (by vehicle)
Wstęp wolny	admission free
Wyprzedaż	sale
Zajęte	engaged/in use
Zamknięte	closed

Polite expressions

There are two forms of address in Polish: formal (**pan/pani** - Mr/Mrs) and informal (**ty**). You should always use the formal until you are invited to use the informal.

Where do you work?	**Gdzie pan/pani pracuje?** gdje pan/**pa**-nee pra-**tsoo**-ye?
Are you English?	**Czy pan/pani jest z Anglii?** chi pan/**pa**-nee yest **z an**-glee?
What's your name?	**Jak się pan/pani nazywa?** yak she pan/**pa**-nee na-**zi**-va?
This is a gift for you	**To prezent dla pana/pani** to **pre**-zent dla **pa**-na/**pa**-nee
Pleased to meet you	**Miło mi poznać** **mee**-wo mee **poz**-nach
The lunch was delicious	**Obiad był doskonały** **o**-byat biw dos-ko-**na**-wi
The dinner was delicious	**Kolacja była doskonała** ko-**lats**-ya **bi**-wa dos-ko-**na**-wa
This is my husband	**To mój mąż** to mooy monsh
This is my wife	**To moja żona** to **mo**-ya **zho**-na

This is my son	**To mój syn** to mooy sin
This is my daughter	**To moja córka** to **mo**-ya **tsoor**-ka
Enjoy your holiday!	**Dobrych wakacji!** **do**-brih va-**ka**-tsee!

Celebrations

In Poland most people celebrate their name-days (**imieniny**), rather than birthdays (**urodziny**), although both occasions can be celebrated. The standard wish on this type of occasion is **wszystkiego najlepszego!** fshist-**kye**-go nay-lep-**she**-go! (all the best) For Easter - **Wielkanoc** - there isn't really a special wish, so people can just say **Wesołych Świąt** (merry holidays) the same as for the Christmas wish.

I'd like to wish (you) all the best!	**Życzę wszystkiego najlepszego!** **zhi**-che fshist-**kye**-go nay-lep-**she**-go!
Cheers/to your health!	**Na zdrowie!** na **zdro**-vye!

Merry Christmas!	**Wesołych świąt!** ve-**so**-wih shfyont!
Happy New Year!	**Szczęśliwego Nowego Roku!** shchen-shlee-**ve**-go no-**ve**-go **ro**-koo!
Happy Easter!	**Wesołych Świąt!** ve-**so**-wih shfyont!
Good luck!	**Powodzenia!** po-vo-**dze**-nya!
Have a good journey!	**Szczęśliwej podróży!** shchen-**shlee**-vey po-**droo**-zhi!
Enjoy your meal!	**Smacznego!** smach-**ne**-go!

Making friends

In this section we have used the familiar form **ty** for the questions. In Polish there is one form of question for first names and another for surnames, although in practice the latter form can be used for both first name and surname.

What's your name? (first name)	**Jak ci na imię?** yak chee na **ee**-mye?
My name is... (first name)	**Na imię mi...** na **ee**-mye mee...
What's your name? (first name/surname)	**Jak się nazywasz?** yak she na-**zi**-vash?
My name is... (first name/ surname)	**Nazywam się...** na-**zi**-vam she...
Where are you from?	**Skąd jesteś?** skont **yes**-tesh?
I am English, from London (a man speaking)	**Jestem Anglikiem, z Londynu** **yes**-tem an-**glee**-kyem, z lon-**di**-noo
I am English (a woman speaking)	**Jestem Angielką** **yes**-tem an-**gyel**-kow
Pleased to meet you!	**Miło mi poznać!** **mee**-wo mee **poz**-nach!
How old are you?	**Ile masz lat?** **ee**-le mash lat?
I'm ... years old	**Mam ... lat** mam ... lat

Where do you live?	**Gdzie mieszkasz?** gdje **myesh**-kash?
Where do you live? (plural)	**Gdzie mieszkacie?** gdje myesh-**ka**-che?
I live in London	**Mieszkam w Londynie** **myesh**-kam v lon-**di**-nye
We live in Glasgow	**Mieszkamy w Glasgow** myesh-**ka**-mi **v glas**-gow
I'm at school	**Chodzę do szkoły** **ho**-dze do **shko**-wi
I work	**Pracuję** pra-**tsoo**-ye
I'm retired	**Jestem na emeryturze** **yes**-tem na e-me-ri-**too**-zhe
I'm...	**Jestem...** **yes**-tem...
married	**żonaty** zho-**na**-ti
divorced	**rozwiedziony** roz-vye-**djo**-ni
widowed (a man speaking)	**wdowcem** **vdof**-tsem
I'm...	**Jestem...** **yes**-tem...
married	**mężatką** men-**zhat**-kow

divorced	**rozwiedziona** roz-vye-**djo**-na
widowed (a woman speaking)	**wdową** **vdo**-vow
I have...	**Mam...** mam...
a boyfriend	**chłopaka** hwo-**pa**-ka
a girlfriend	**dziewczynę** djev-**chi**-ne
a partner (man/woman)	**partnera/partnerkę** part-**ne**-ra/par-**tner**-ke
I have ... children	**Mam ... dzieci** mam ... **dje**-chee
I don't have children	**Nie mam dzieci** nye mam **dje**-chee
I'm here...	**Jestem tu...** **yes**-tem too...
on holiday	**na wakcjach** na va-**kats**-yah
on business	**służbowo** swoozh-**bo**-vo
for the weekend	**na weekend** na **week**-end

> **Leisure/interests** (p 84) > **Sport** (p 89)

Work

What do you do?	**Gdzie pan/pani pracuje?** gdje pan/**pa**-nee pra-**tsoo**-ye?
Do you like your job? (formal)	**Czy lubi pan/pani swoją pracę?** chi **loo**-bi pan/**pa**-nee **sfo**-yow **pra**-tse?
I'm...	**Jestem...** **yes** tem...
a doctor	**lekarzem** le-**ka**-zhem
a manager	**kierownikiem** kye rov-**nee**-kyem
a housewife	**gospodynią domową** gos-po-**di n**-yow do-**mo** vow
I work from home	**Pracuję w domu** pra-**tsoo**-ye **v do**-moo
I'm self-employed	**Pracuję dla siebie** pra-**tsoo**-ye dla **she**-bye

Weather

Prognoza pogody prog-**no**-za po-**go**-di	weather forecast
Zmienna pogoda **zmyen**-na po-**go**-da	changeable weather
Ładna pogoda **wad**-na po-**go**-da	fine weather
Zła pogoda zwa po-**go**-da	bad weather
Pochmurno poh-**moor**-no	cloudy
Słonecznie swo-**nech**-nye	sunny

It's sunny	**Jest słońce** yest **swon**-tse
It's raining	**Pada deszcz** **pa**-da deshch
It's snowing	**Pada śnieg** **pa**-da shnyek
It's windy	**Jest wiatr** yest vyatr
What lovely weather!	**Ale piękna pogoda!** a-le **p yen**-kna po-**go**-da!

What awful weather!	**Ale okropna pogoda!** a-le o-**krop**-na po-**go**-da!
What will the weather be like tomorrow?	**Jaka pogoda będzie jutro?** ya-ka po-**go**-da **ben**-dje **yoo**-tro?
Is it going to rain?	**Czy będzie padać?** chi **ben**-dje **pa**-dach?
It's very hot/cold today	**Dzisiaj jest bardzo gorąco/zimno** **djee**-shay yest **bar**-dzo go-**ron**-tso/**zheem**-no
Will there be a storm?	**Czy będzie burza?** chi **ben**-dje **boo**-zha?
Do you think it will snow?	**Czy będzie padać śnieg?** chi **ben**-dje **pa**-dach shnyek?
Will it be foggy?	**Czy będzie mgła?** chi **ben**-dje mgwa?
What is the temperature?	**Jaka jest temperatura?** **ya**-ka yest tem-pe-ra-**too**-ra?

Getting around

Asking the way

Naprzeciwko na-pshe-**cheef**-ko	opposite
Obok **o**-bok	next to
Blisko **blees**-ko	near to
Światła **shfya**-twa	traffic lights
Skrzyżowanie skshi-zho-**va**-nye	crossroads
Róg rook	corner
Za rogiem za **ro**-gyem	round the corner
Na rogu na **ro**-goo	at the corner

FACE TO FACE

A **Przepraszam, jak dojść do dworca?**
pshe-**pra**-sham, yak doyshch do **dvor**-tsa?
Excuse me, how do I get (on foot) to the station?

B **Prosto, za kościołem skręcić w lew/w prawo**
pros-to za kosh-**cho**-wem **skren**-cheech v **le**-vo/ f **pra**-vo
Keep straight on, after the church turn left/right

A **Czy to daleko?**
chi to da-**le**-ko?
Is it far?

B **Nie, 200 metrów/pięć minut**
nye, dvyesh-che **met**-roof/pyench **mee**-noot
No, 200 metres/five minutes

A **Dziękuję!**
djen-**koo**-ye!
Thank you!

B **Proszę bardzo**
pro-she **bar**-dzo
You're welcome

We're lost	**Zgubiliśmy się** zgoo-bee-**leesh**-mi she
We're looking for...	**Szukamy...** shoo-**ka**-mi...

Is this the right way to...? (on foot)	**Czy tędy dojdzie się do...?** chi **ten**-di **doy**-dje she do...?
How do I/we get (on foot/ by transport)	**Jak dojść/dojechać** yak doyshch/do-**ye**-hach
onto the motorway?	**do autostrady?** do au-to-**stra**-di?
to the museum?	**do muzeum?** do **moo**-ze-oom?
to the shops?	**do sklepów?** do **skle**-poof?
Can I see it on the map?	**Czy można zobaczyć na mapie?** chi **mozh**-na zo-**ba**-chich na **ma**-pye?

YOU MAY HEAR...

Prosto **pro**-sto	straight on
skręcić w lewo **skren**-chich **v le**-vo	turn left
skręcić w prawo **skren**-chich **f pra**-vo	turn right
Daleko da-**le**-ko	far

Blisko **blees**-ko	near
Kawałek ka-**va**-wek	a little bit
Pół godziny piechotą poow go-**djee**-ni pye-**ho**-tow	half an hour on foot
autobusem au-to-**boo**-sem	by bus
pociągiem po-**chon**-gyem	by train

Bus and coach

In cities you can buy tickets from kiosks and in some post offices, as well as from some bus drivers. To validate them you must punch them in the machine on board the bus or tram. Warsaw is the only city which has a metro and this is in the process of being extended. An integrated system exists which allows you to use the same kind of ticket for all three means of transport.

FACE TO FACE

A **Przepraszam, który autobus jedzie do centrum?**
pshe-**pra**-sham, **ktoo**-ri au-**to**-boos **ye**-dje do **tsen**-troom?
Excuse me, which bus goes to the centre?

B **Numer 15**
noo-mer pyen-**tnash**-che
Number 15

A **Gdzie jest przystanek autobusowy?**
gdje yest pshi-**sta**-nek au-to-boo-**so**-vi?
Where is the bus stop?

B **Tam na prawo**
tam na **pra**-vo
There, on the right

A **Gdzie można kupić bilety?**
gdje **mozh**-na **koo**-peech bee-**le**-ti?
Where can I buy the tickets?

B **W kiosku**
f kyos-koo
At the kiosk

Is there a bus/tram to...? — **Czy jest autobus/tramwaj do...?**
chi yest au-**to**-boos/**tram**-vay do...?

Where do I catch the bus/tram to...?	**Skąd jedzie autobus/ tramwaj do...?** skont **ye**-dje au-**to**-boos/ **tram**-vay do...?
We're going to...	**Jedziemy do...** ye-**dje**-mi do...
How much is it to go...?	**Ile kosztuje bilet...?** **ee**-le kosh-**too**-ye **bee**-let...?
to the centre	**do centrum** do **tsen**-troom
to the beach	**na plażę** na **pla**-zhe
How often are the buses to...?	**Jak często są autobusy do...?** yak **chen**-sto sow au-to-**boo**-si do...?
When is the first/ the last bus to...?	**Kiedy jest pierwszy/ostatni autobus do...?** **kye**-di yest **pyer**-fshi/os-**tat**-nee au-**to**-boos do...?
Please tell me when to get off	**Proszę mi powiedzieć kiedy wysiąść** **pro**-she mee po-**vye**-djech **kye**-di **vi**-shonshch
I'm getting off now	**Ja teraz wysiadam** ya **te**-ras vi-**sha**-dam

This is my stop	**To mój przystanek** to mooy pshis-**ta**-nek

YOU MAY HEAR...

To pani/pana przystanek to **pa**-nee/**pa**-na pshis-**tan**-ek	This is your stop
lepiej jechać autobusem **le**-pyey **ye**-hach au-to-**boo**-sem	It's better to take the bus

Metro

The only city with a metro system is Warsaw. You pay a flat rate for each journey. You can save by buying a one-day ticket, or a ticket valid for a few days. For single journeys it is practical to obtain a larger number of tickets, for instance, a booklet of 10.

Wejście **vey**-shche	entrance
Wyjście **viy**-shche	way out/exit
Bilet całodobowy **bee**-let tsa-wo-do-**bo**-vi	a 24 hour ticket

A book of (10) tickets, please	**Proszę dziesięć biletów** **pro**-she **dje**-shench bee-**le**-toof
With concession/ normal	**Ulgowych/normalnych** ool-**go**-vih/nor-**mal**-nih
Where is the nearest stop?	**Gdzie jest najbliższy przystanek?** gdje yest nay-**bleesh**-shi pshis-**ta**-nek?
I'm going to...	**Jadę do...** **ya**-de do...?
Do you have a map of the metro?	**Czy jest mapa metra?** chi yest **ma**-pa **me**-tra?
How do I get to...?	**Jak dojechać do...?** yak do-**ye**-hach do...?
Do I have to change?	**Czy muszę się przesiąść?** chi **moo**-she she **pshe**-shonshch?
What is the next stop?	**Jaki jest następny przystanek?** **ya**-kee yest na-**stemp**-ni pshi-**sta**-nek?
Excuse me!	**Przepraszam!** pshe-**pra**-sham!
This is my stop	**To mój przystanek** to mooy pshi-**sta**-nek
I'm getting off now	**Ja teraz wysiadam** ya **te**-ras vi-**sha**-dam

> **Luggage** (p 108)

Train

The Polish rail network is operated by the state-owned **PKP - Polskie Koleje Państwowe**. Travelling by train is cheaper than in Britain. Train fares differ depending on the distance and the type of train. Most trains have compartments. A first class seat costs 50% more than second class. When booking you should always check to see if the train you want to travel on requires reservations, as without a reservation it might be difficult to find a seat. All fast trains require reservations. The fastest connection is between Warsaw and Kraków. You can buy tickets using a credit card only at designated ticket desks at the station, otherwise you pay cash.

Pociąg podmiejski **po**-chonk pod-**myey**-skee	a slow local train (stops at all stations)
Pociąg pospieszny **po**-chonk pos-**pyesh**-ni	fast train (stops at some stations)
Expres **eks**-pres	express (stops at main stations only)

Getting around

IC – Intercity een-ter-**see**-tee	equivalent to European IC trains
EC – Eurocity ee-see – **e**-oo-ro-**see**-tee	as above
Pociąg Międzynarodowy **po**-chonk myen-dzi-na-ro-**do**-vi	International Train
TLK Tanie Linie Kolejowe **ta**-nye **lee**-nye ko-le-**yo**-ve	Cheap Railway Lines
Dworzec Kolejowy *or* **Dworzec PKP** **dvo**-zhets ko-le-**yo**-vi *or* **dvo**-zhets pe-ka-pe	railway station
Peron **pe**-ron	platform
Tor tor	track at the platform
Kasa biletowa **ka**-sa bee-le-**to**-va	ticket office
Rozkład jazdy **ros**-kwat **yaz**-di	timetable
Opóźniony o-poozh-**nyo**-ni	delayed
Przechowalnia bagażu pshe-ho-**val**-nya ba-**ga**-zhoo	left luggage

FACE TO FACE

A **Kiedy jest następny pociąg do...?**
kye-di yest nas-**tem**-pni **po**-chonk do...?
When is the next train to...?

B **O 17.00**
o she-dem-**nas**-tey
At 17.00

A **Proszę 3 bilety**
pro-she tshi bee-**le**-ti
I'd like 3 tickets, please

B **W jedną stronę czy powrotne?**
v yed-now **stro**-ne chi po-**vrot**-ne?
Singles or returns?

one ticket	**jeden bilet** **ye**-den **bee**-let
two tickets	**dwa bilety** dva bee-**le**-ti
to...	**do ...** do ...
first/second class	**pierwsza/druga klasa** **pyerf**-sha/**droo**-ga **kla**-sa

smoking/ non-smoking	**dla palących/ dla niepalących** dla pa-**lon**-tsih/ dla **nye**-pa-lon-tsih
Is there a supplement to pay?	**Czy jest dodatkowa opłata?** chi yest do-dat-**ko**-va op-**wa**-ta?
I want to book a reserved seat on the express train to Warsaw	**Proszę bilet z miejscówką na pociąg ekspresowy do Warszawy** **pro**-she **bee**-let z myeys-**tsoof**-kow na **po**-chonk eks-pre-**so**-vi do var-**sha**-vi
Do I have to change?	**Czy muszę się przesiąść?** chi **moo**-she she **pshe**-shonch?
How long do I have to wait for the next train?	**Jak długo muszę czekać na następny pociąg?** yak **dwoo**-go **mu**-she **che**-kach na nas-**tem**-pni **po**-chonk?
Which platform does it leave from?	**Z którego peronu on odjeżdża?** s ktoo-**re**-go pe-**ro**-noo on od-**yezh**-dja?
Is this the train for...?	**Czy to pociąg do...?** chi to **po**-chonk do...?

Why is the train delayed?	**Dlaczego pociąg jest opóźniony?** dla-**che**-go **po**-chonk yest o-poozh-**n yo**-ni?
When will it leave?	**Kiedy pociąg odjeżdża?** **k ye**-di **po**-chonk od-**yezh**-dja?
Does it stop at...?	**Czy zatrzymuje się w...?** chi za-tshi-**moo**-ye she v...?
When does it arrive in...?	**Kiedy jest w...?** **kye**-di yest v...?
Please tell me when we get to...	**Proszę mi powiedzieć kiedy dojedziemy do...** **pro**-she mee po-**vye**-djech **kye**-di do-ye-**dje**-mi do...
Is there a restaurant car?	**Czy jest wagon restauracyjny?** chi yest **va**-gon res-tau-ra-**tsiy**-ni?
Is this seat free?	**Czy to miejsce jest wolne?** chi to **myey**-stse yest **vol**-ne?
Excuse me! (to get past)	**Przepraszam!** pshe-**pra**-sham!

> **Luggage** (p 108)

Taxi

The easiest place to find a taxi stand is at a railway station. Official taxis are generally marked with a recognised taxi company name.

I want a taxi	**Chcę taksówkę** htse ta-**ksoof**-ke
Where can I get a taxi?	**Gdzie są taksówki?** gdje sow tak-**ksoof**-kee?
Please order me a taxi...	**Proszę zamówić taksówkę dla mnie...** **pro**-she za-**moo**-veech tak-**soof**-ke dla mnye...
now	**teraz** **te**-ras
for...(time)	**na ... godzinę** na ... go-**djee**-ne
How much will it cost to go...?	**Ile kosztuje przejazd...?** **ee**-le kosh-**too**-ye **pshe**-yazd...?
to the station	**na dworzec** na **dvo**-zhets
to the airport	**na lotnisko** na lot-**nees**-ko

to this address	**na ten adres** na ten **ad**-res
How much is it?	**Ile kosztuje?** **ee**-le kosh-**too**-ye?
Why is it so much?	**Dlaczego tak drogo?** dla-**che**-go tak **dro**-go?
It's more than on the meter	**Jest więcej niż na liczniku** yest **vyen**-tsey neesh na leech-**nee**-koo
Keep the change	**Reszta dla pana/pani** **resh**-ta dla **pa**-na/**pa**-nee
Sorry, I don't have any change	**Przepraszam, nie mam drobnych** pshe-**pra**-sham, nye mam **drob**-nih
I'm in a hurry	**Spieszę się** **spye**-she she
Can you go a little faster?	**Czy można jechać szybciej?** chi **mozh**-na **ye**-hach **ship**-chey?
I have to catch...	**Muszę zdążyć na...** **moo**-she **zdon**-zhich na...
a train	**pociąg** **po**-chonk
a plane	**samolot** sa-**mo**-lot

> **Luggage** (p 108)

Boat and ferry

There is a frequent ferry service throughout the year to Sweden from the major ports in **Świnoujście**, **Gdańsk** and **Gdynia**.

How much is a ... ticket?	**Ile kosztuje ... bilet?** **ee**-le kosh-**too**-ye ... **bee**-let?
single	**w jedną stronę** **v yed**-now **stro**-ne
return	**powrotny** pov-**rot**-ni
How much is it for a car and ... people?	**Ile kosztuje jeden samochód i ... osoby?** **ee**-le kosh-**too**-ye **ye**-den sa-**mo**-hoot ee ... o-**so**-bi?
Where does the ferry leave from?	**Skąd odpływa prom?** skont ot-**pwi**-va prom?
for...	**do...** do...
When is the first/ last boat?	**Kiedy jest pierwszy prom/ ostatni prom?** **kye** di yest **pyerf**-shi prom/ os-**tat**-nee prom?

I'd like to reserve a cabin for three people	**Chcę zarezerwować kabinę na trzy osoby** htse za-re-zer-**vo**-vach ka-**bee**-ne na tshi o-**so**-bi

YOU MAY HEAR...

To jest ostatni prom to yest os-**tat**-nee prom	This is the last boat
Dzisiaj nie kursuje **djee**-shay nye koor-**soo**-ye	There is no service today

Air travel

port lotniczy/lotnisko port lot-**nee**-chi/lot-**nees**-ko	airport
przyloty pshi-**lo**-ti	arrivals
odloty od-**lo**-ti	departures
loty krajowe **lo**-ti kra-**yo**-ve	domestic flights
loty międzynarodowe **lo**-ti myen-dzi-na-ro-**do**-ve	international flights
wyjście do samolotu **viy**-shche do sa-mo-**lo**-too	boarding gate

karta pokładowa **kar**-ta po-kwa-**do**-va	boarding card
odprawa ot-**pra**-va	check-in

Excuse me, how do I get to the airport?	**Przepraszam, jak dojechać na lotnisko?** pshe-**pra**-sham, yak do-**ye**-hach na lot-**nees**-ko?
Excuse me, is there a bus to the airport?	**Czy jest autobus na lotnisko?** chi yest au-**to**-boos na lot-**nees**-ko?
Where is the luggage for the flight from...?	**Gdzie jest odbiór bagażu z...?** gdje yest **od**-byoor ba-**ga**-zhoo z...?
Where can I change some money?	**Gdzie mogę wymienić pieniądze?** gdje **mo**-ge vi-**mye**-neech pye-**nyon**-dze?
How do I/we get into town?	**Jak dojechać do miasta?** yak do-**ye**-hach do **myas**-ta?
How much is it by taxi...?	**Ile kosztuje dojazd taksówką...?** **ee**-le kosh-**too**-ye **do**-yazd tak-**soof**-kow...?

> **Luggage** (p 108)

to go into town?	**do miasta?** do **myas**-ta?
to go to the Hotel...?	**do hotelu...?** do ho-**te**-loo...?

YOU MAY HEAR...

Wejście do samolotu nastąpi przy wyjściu numer... **ve**y-shche do sa-mo-**lo**-too nas-**tom**-pee phsi **viy**-schchoo **noo**-mer...	Boarding will take place at gate number...
Proszę przechodzić do wyjścia numer... **pro**-she pshe-**ho**-djeech do **viy**-shcha **noo**-mer...	Go to gate number...

Customs control

With the Single European Market, EU citizens are subject only to highly selective spot-checks and they can pass through customs with the sign **Nic do zgłoszenia** (unless they have goods to declare - **Towary do zgłoszenia**). There are no restrictions, either by quantity or value, on goods purchased by EU travellers in other EU countries, provided that they are for their own personal use. If you are unsure of certain items, check with the customs officials as to whether duty – **cło** – is payable.

mieszkańcy UE myesh-**kan**-tsi oo-e	EU citizens
inne kraje **eén**-ne **kra**-ye	other passports
dowód osobisty **do**-voot o-so-**bees**-ti	identity card
cło tswo	customs duty

Do I have to pay duty on this?	**Czy muszę zapłacić cło?** chi **moo**-she za-**pwa**-cheech tswo?
It's for my own personal use/ for a present	**To do użytku osobistego/ na prezent** to do oo-**zhit**-koo o-so-bees-**te**-go/na **pre**-zent
We are on our way to... (if in transit through a country)	**Jesteśmy tranzytem...** yes-**tesh**-mi tran-**zi**-tem...
The child is/ children are on this passport	**Dziecko jest/dzieci są w paszporcie** **djets**-ko yest/**dje**-chee sow f pash-**por**-che

Getting around

Driving

Car hire

Car rental in Poland is quite expensive, but Polish and international rental agencies are well represented at airports, railway stations and major hotels.

prawo jazdy **pra**-vo **yaz**-di	driving licence
ubezpieczenie auto-casco oo-bes-pye-**che**-nye au-to-**kas**-ko	fully comprehensive insurance

I would like to hire a car for ... days (man speaking/ woman speaking, respectively)	**chciałbym/chciałabym wynająć samochód na ... dni** **hchaw**-bim/**hcha**-wa-bim vi-**na**-yonch sa-**mo**-hoot na ... dnee
What are your rates...?	**Ile kosztuje...?** **ee**-le kosh-**too**-ye...?

per day	**dzziennie** **djen**-nye
per week	**na tydzień** na **ti**-djen
How much is the deposit?	**Ile wynosi depozyt?** **ee**-le vi-**no**-shee de-**po**-zit?
Do you take credit cards?	**Czy można zapłacić kartą?** chi **mozh**-na za-**pwa**-cheech **kar**-tow?
Is there a mileage (kilometre) charge?	**Czy zapłata jest od kilometra?** chi za-**pwa**-ta yest ot kee-lo-**met**-ra?
How much is it?	**Ile wynosi?** **ee**-le **vi** no-shee?
Does the price include fully comprehensive insurance?	**Czy ubezpeczenie autocasko jest wliczone w opłatę?** chi oo-bes-pye-**che**-nye au-to-kas-ko yest vlee-**cho**-ne v op-**wa**-te?
Must I return the car here?	**Czy muszę oddać samochód tutaj?** chi **moo**-she **od**-dach sa-**mo**-hoot **too**-tay?
By what time?	**Do której godziny?** do **ktoo**-rey go-**djee**-ni?

YOU MAY HEAR...

Proszę oddać samochód z pełnym zbiornikiem pro-she od-dach sa-mo-hoot s pew-nim zbyor-nee-kyem	Please return the car with a full tank

Driving and petrol

The speed limits in Poland are compatible with the rules in the EU countries, and are as follows: 60 km/h (37) in built up areas, 90 km/h (56) on main roads, and 110 km/h (68) on motorways. A breakdown service - **Pomoc Drogowa** - is available, and there are plenty of petrol stations. Main roads are generally good, while the smaller country roads are not as well maintained. The alcohol limit is much lower than in Britain - 0.02%. Between October and February headlights must be switched on at all times while driving.

Can I/we park here?	**Czy można tu zaparkować?** chi **mozh**-na too za-par-**ko**-vach?

How long for?	**Na jak długo?** na yak **dwoo**-go?
Which exit is it for...?	**Który zjazd do...?** **ktoo**-ri z yazd do...?
Do I/we need snow chains?	**Czy potrzeba łańcuchów na opony?** chi pot-**she**-ba wan-**tsoo**-hoof na o-**po**-ni?

International petrol stations accept major credit cards, however, Polish companies usually request payment in cash.

benzyna ben-**zi**-na	petrol
super **soo**-per	4 star
czerwona 98 cher-**vo**-na 98 dje-vyen-**dje**-shont **o**-shem	premium
zielona super 98 zhe-**lo**-na **soo**-per dje-vyen-**dje**-shont **o**-shem	premium
żółta 94 **zhoow**-ta dje-vyen-**dje**-shont **chte**-ri	regular

zielona 95 zhe-**lo**-na dje-vyen-**dje**-shont **chte**-ri	regular
dizel **dee**-zel	diesel
bezołowiowa bez-o-wo-**vyo**-va	unleaded

Fill it up, please	**Do pełna, proszę** do **pew**-na, **pro**-she
Please check the oil/water	**proszę sprawdzić olej/wodę** **pro**-she **sprav**-djeech **o**-ley/**vo**-de
...60 zł. worth of unleaded petrol	**...bezołowiowej za 60 zł.** ...bez-o-wo-**vyo**-vey za shesh-**dje**-shont **zwo**-tih
Where is the...?	**Gdzie jest...?** gdje yest...?
air line	**powietrze** po-**vyet**-she
water	**woda** **vo**-da
Pump number...	**Pompa numer...** **pom**-pa **noo**-mer...
Where do I pay?	**Gdzie płacę?** gdje **pwa**-tse?

Can I pay by card? **Czy mogę zapłacić kartą?**
chi **mo**-ge za-**pwa**-cheech **kar**-tow?

YOU MAY HEAR...	
Potrzeba trochę oleju/ trochę wody po-**tshe**-ba **tro**-he o-**le**-yoo **tro**-he **vo**-di	You need some oil/ some water
Wszystko w porządku **fshis**-tko f po-**zhon**-tkoo	Everything is OK

Breakdown

If you break down, the emergency phone number for the Polish equivalent of the AA, **Pomoc Drogowa**, is **981**. For the Breakdown service telephone **+(48-61) 831 98 00**. Breakdown services are provided by the Polish Motoring Association (**PZMot**) and usually only cash payments are accepted.

Can you help me? (plural you)	**Czy możecie pomóc?** chi mo-**zhe**-che **po**-moots?
My car has broken down	**Zepsuł mi się samochód** **zep**-soow mee she sa-**mo**-hoot
I've run out of petrol	**Benzyna mi się skończyła** ben-**zi**-na mee she skon-**chi**-wa
Can you tow me?	**Czy możecie mnie zaholować?** chi mo-**zhe**-che mnye za-ho-**lo**-vach?
Do you have parts for a (make of car) ...?	**Czy są części do...?** chi sow **chen**-shchee do...?
There's something wrong here...	**Tu coś nie działa...** too tsosh nye **dja**-wa...
Can you replace...?	**Czy można wymienić...?** chi **mozh**-na vi-**mye**-neech...?

Car parts

The ... doesn't work	...**nie działa** ...nye **dja**-wa
The ... don't work	...**nie działają** ...nye dja-**wa**-yow

accelerator	**pedał gazu**	**pe**-daw **ga**-zoo
alternator	**alternator**	al-ter-**na**-tor
battery	**akumulator**	a-koo-moo-**la**-tor
bonnet	**maska**	**mas**-ka
brakes	**hamulce**	ha-**mool**-tse
choke	**dławik**	**dwa**-veek
clutch	**sprzęgło**	**spshen**-gwo
distributor	**rozdzielacz**	roz-**dje**-lach
engine	**silnik**	**sheel**-neek
exhaust	**rura wydechowa**	**roo**-ra vi-de-**ho**-va
fuse	**bezpiecznik**	bes-**pyech**-neek
gears	**biegi**	**bye**-gee
handbrake	**hamulec ręczny**	ha-**moo**-lets **ren**-ch-ni
headlights	**reflektory**	ref-lek-**to**-ri
ignition	**zapłon**	**zap**-won
indicator	**kierunkowskaz**	kye-roon-**kof**-skas

points	**styki**	**sti**-kee
radiator	**chłodnica**	hwod-**nee**-tsa
reverse gear	**bieg wsteczny**	byeg **fstech**-ni
seat belt	**pas**	pas
spark plug	**świeca zapłonowa**	**shfye**-tsa za-pwo-**no**-va
steering wheel	**kierownica**	kye-rov-**nee**-tsa
steering	**kierowanie**	kye-ro-**va**-nye
wheel	**koło**	**ko**-wo
windscreen	**szyba przednia/ okno**	**shi**-ba **phed**-nya/ **ok**-no
windscreen wiper	**wycieraczka szyby**	vi-che-**rach**-ka **shi**-bi

Car parts

Road signs

śliska jezdnia
slippery road

niebezpieczne pobocze
bad side space of roads

uwaga na dzieci
children on the road

przejście dla pieszych
pedestrians crossing

wypadek
accident

inne niebezpieczeństwo
danger

north

Północ

west Zachód Wschód east

Południe

south

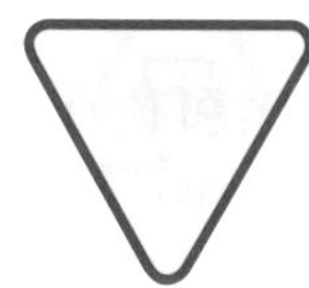

ustąp pierwszeństwa przejazdu
give way

autostrada
motorway

zakaz ruchu w obu kierunkach
any kind of traffic prohibited

Staying somewhere

Hotel (booking)

Tourism in Poland is a fast developing industry. You can find all the necessary information at **www.poland-tourism.pl**. Agritourism is worth considering, and there are more and more B&B farms in beautiful rural areas: **www.agritourism.pl**.

Pokój jednoosobowy **po**-kooy ye-dno-o-so-**bo**-vi	single room
Pokój dwuosobowy **po**-kooy dvoo-o-so-**bo**-vi	double room
Z wygodami z vi-go-**da**-mee	with private facilities
Liczba osób dorosłych **leech**-ba **o**-soop do-ros-wih	number of adults
liczba dzieci **leech**-ba **dje**-chee	number of children

FACE TO FACE

A **Chciałbym/chciałabym zarezerwować pokój jednoosobowy/dwuosobowy**
hchaw-bim/**hcha**-wa-bim za-re-zer-**vo**-vach **po**-kooy ye-dno-o-so-**bo**-vi/dvoo-o-so-**bo**-vi
I'd like to book a single/double room

B **Na ile nocy?**
na **ee**-le **no**-tsi?
For how many nights?

A **na jedną noc.../dwie noce/od ... do ...**
na **yed**-now nots.../dvye **no**-tse/ot ... do ...
for one night/two nights/from ... to ...

Do you have a room for tonight?	**Czy jest wolny pokój na tą noc?** chi yest **vol**-ni **po**-kooy na tow nots?
with a bath	**z łazienką** z wa-**zhen**-kow
with a shower	**z prysznicem** s prish-**nee**-tsem
with a double bed	**z podwójnym łóżkiem** s pod-**vooy**-nim **woosh**-kyem
with twin beds	**z dwoma łóżkami** s dvo-ma woosh-**ka**-mi

with an extra bed for a child	**z dodatkowym łóżeczkiem dla dziecka** z do-dat-**ko**-vim woo-**zhech**-kyem dla **djets**-ka
How much is it per night/ per week?	**Ile kosztuje jedna noc/ jeden tydzień?** **ee**-le kosh-**too**-ye **yed**-na nots/ **ye**-den **ti**-djen?
Is breakfast included?	**Razem ze śniadaniem?** **ra**-zem ze shnya-**da**-nyem?
Have you anything cheaper?	**Czy jest coś tańszego?** chi yest tsosh tan-**she**-go?
I'd like to see the room	**czy można zobaczyć pokój?** chi **mozh**-na zo-**ba**-chich **po**-kooy?

YOU MAY HEAR...

Nie mamy nic wolnego nye **ma**-mi neets vol-**ne**-go	We're full
Nazwisko proszę naz-**vees**-ko **pro**-she	Your name, please
Proszę potwierdzić **pro**-she pot-**fyer**-djeech	Please confirm...

przez e-mail pshez e-mail	by e-mail
faksem fa-xem	by fax

Many hotels are now signposted in towns. The Polish word for a hotel is the same as in English, with the stress over the first syllable: **ho**tel.

I booked a room	**Mam zarezerwowany pokój** mam za-re-zervo-**va**-ni **po**-kooy
in the name of...	**na nazwisko...** na naz-**vees**-ko...
Where can I park the car?	**Gdzie mogę zaparkować samochód?** gdje **mo**-ge za-par-**ko**-vach sa-**mo**-hoot?
What time is...?	**O której godzinie jest...?** o **ktoo**-rey go-**djee**-nye yest...?
dinner	**obiad** **ob**-yat
breakfast	**śniadanie** shnya-**da**-nye
The key, please	**Proszę klucz** **pro**-she klooch

Room number...	**Numer pokoju** **noo**-mer po-**ko**-yoo
Are there any messages for me?	**Czy jest dla mnie jakaś wiadomość?** chi yest dla mnye **ya**-kash vya-**do**-moshch?
Can I send a fax?	**Czy mogę wysłać fax?** chi **mo**-ge **vis**-wach fax?
I'm leaving tomorrow	**Jutro wyjeżdżam** **yoo**-tro vi-**yezh**-djam
Please prepare the bill	**Proszę wystawić rachunek** **pro**-she vis-**ta**-veech ra-**hoo**-nek

Camping

Camping is popular and there are a lot of campsites in Poland.

śmieci shmye-chee	rubbish
woda pitna **vo**-da **peet**-na	drinking water
gniazdko **gnyas**-tko	electric point

palenie ognia wzbronione pa-**le**-nye **og**-nya wzbro-**nyo**-ne	no fires

Is there a restaurant/self-service café on the campsite?	**Czy jest restauracja/bar samoobsługowy na kempingu?** czy yest re-stau-**ra**-tsya/bar sa-mo-ops-woo-**go**-vi na kem-**peen**-goo?
Do you have any vacancies?	**Czy są wolne miejsca?** chi sow **vol**-ne **myey**-stsa?
How much is it...?	**Ile kosztuje...?** **ee**-le kosh-**too**-ye...?
per night	**za noc** za nots
per tent	**za namiot** za **na**-myot
per caravan	**za przyczepę** za pshi-**che**-pe
per person	**od osoby** od o-**so**-bi

Does the price include...?	**czy w tej cenie jest...?** chi f tey **tse**-nye yest...?
showers/hot water/electricity	**prysznic/gorąca woda/ elektryczność** **prish**-neets/go-**ron**-tsa **vo**-da/ e-lek-**trich**-noshch
We'd like to stay for ... nights	**Chcielibyśmy zatrzymać się na ... noce/nocy** **hche**-lee-bish-mi za-**tshi**-mach she na ... **no**-tse/no-tsi

Self-catering

There are plenty of self-catering apartments and houses to rent.

Who do we contact if there are problems?	**Z kim można się skontaktować w razie problemów?** s keem **mozh**-na she skon-tak-**to**-vach **v ra**-zhe pro-**ble**-moof?
How does the heating work?	**Jak działa ogrzewanie?** yak **dja**-wa og-zhe-**va**-nye?

Is there always hot water?	**Czy zawsze jest gorąca woda?** chi **zaf**-she yest go-**ron**-tsa **vo**-da?
Where is the nearest supermarket?	**Gdzie jest najbliższy supermarket?** gdje yest nay-**bleesh**-shi **soo**-per-mar-ket?
Where do we leave the rubbish?	**Gdzie można zostawić śmieci?** gdje **mozh**-na zo-**sta**-veech **shmye**-chee?

> **Sightseeing and tourist office** (p 82)

Shopping

Shopping phrases

Shop opening hours are usually from 10.00 am to 6.30 pm, Monday to Friday, with shorter hours on Saturdays. However, many food stores are open from early morning until late at night throughout the week and it's easy to find a few smaller food stores that are open 24 hours a day.

FACE TO FACE

A Czym mogę służyć *or* **Co dla pana/pani?**
chim **mo**-ge **swoo**-zhich *or* tso dla **pa**-na/**pa**-nee?
What would you like?

B Czy jest/czy są...?
chi yest/chi sow...?
Do you have...?

A Tak, oczywiście. Czy jeszcze coś?
tak o-chi-**veesh**-che. chi **yesh**-che tsosh?
Certainly, here you are. Anything else?

Where is...?	**Gdzie jest...?** gdje yest...?
I'm just looking	**Tylko oglądam** **til**-ko og-**lon**-dam
I'm looking for a present for...	**Szukam prezentu dla...** **shoo**-kam pre-**zen**-too dla...
my mother	**mojej mamy** **mo**-yey **ma**-mi
a child	**dziecka** **djets**-ka
Where can I buy...?	**Gdzie mogę kupić...?** gdje **mo**-ge **koo**-peech...?
shoes	**buty** **boo**-ti
gifts	**upominki?** oo-po-**meen**-kee?
Do you have anything...?	**Czy jest/są...?** chi yest/sow...?
larger	**większe** **vyenk**-she
smaller	**mniejsze** **mnyey**-she
It's too expensive for me	**Trochę za drogo dla mnie** **tro**-he za **dro**-go dla mnye
Can you give me a discount?	**Czy można obniżyć cenę?** chi **mozh**-na ob-**nee**-zhich **tse**-ne?

Shops

wyprzedaż vi-pshe-dash	sale
obniżka ob-neesh-ka	discount
nieczynne w czasie wakacji nye-**chin**-ne f cha-she va-**ka**-tsee	closed for holidays

baker's	**piekarnia**	pye-**kar**-nya
butcher's	**rzeźnik**	**zhezh**-neek
cake shop	**cukierniczy**	tsoo-kyer-**nee**-chi
chemist's	**drogeria**	dro-**ger**-ya
clothes	**odzież**	**o**-djesh
fruit and vegetables	**owoce i warzywa**	o-**vo**-tse ee va-**zhi**-va
gifts	**upominki/ prezenty**	oo-po-**meen**-kee/ pre-**zen**-ti
grocer's	**sklep spożywczy**	sklep spo-**zhif**-chi
hairdresser's	**fryzjer**	**friz**-yer
newsagent's	**kiosk**	kyosk
optician's	**optyk**	op-**tich**
perfume shop	**perfumeria**	per-foo-**mer**-ya

pharmacy (for medicines)	**apteka**	ap-**te**-ka
photographic shop	**fotograficzny**	fo-to-gra-**feech**-ni
shoe shop	**obuwie**	o-**boo**-vye
sports shop	**sportowy**	spor-**to**-vi
tobacconist's	**tytoniowy**	ti-to-**nyo**-vi
toys	**zabawki**	za-**baf**-kee

Food (general)

bakery products	**pieczywo**	pye-**chi**-vo
biscuits	**herbatniki**	her-bat-**nee**-kee
bread	**chleb**	hlep
bread roll	**bułka**	**boo**-wka
butter	**masło**	**mas**-wo
cheese	**ser**	ser
chicken	**kurczak**	**koor**-chak
coffee (filter)	**kawa parzona**	ka-va pa-**zho**-na
coffee (instant)	**kawa rozpuszczalna**	**ka**-va ros-push-**chal**-na
cream	**śmietanka**	shmye-**tan**-ka
crisps	**chipsy**	**cheep**-si

eggs	**jajka**	**yay**-ka
fish	**ryby**	**ri**-bi
ham (cooked)	**szynka gotowana**	**shin**-ka go-to-**va**-na
ham (cured)	**szynka wędzona**	**shin**-ka wen-**dzo**-na
herbal tea	**herbata ziołowa**	her-**ba**-ta zho-**wo**-va
jam	**dżem**	djem
orange juice	**sok pomarań-czowy**	sok po-ma-ran-**cho**-vi
margarine	**margaryna**	mar-ga-**ri**-na
marmalade	**marmolada**	mar-mo-**la**-da
milk	**mleko**	**mle**-ko
olive oil	**oliwa**	o-**lee**-va
pepper (condiment)	**pieprz**	pyepsh
salt	**sól**	sool
sugar	**cukier**	**tsoo**-kyer
tea	**herbata**	her-**ba**-ta
tomatoes (tin)	**pomidory w puszce**	po-mee-**do**-ri **f** **poosh**-tse
vinegar	**ocet**	**o**-tset
yoghurt	**jogurt**	**yo**-gurt

> **Measurements and quantities** (p 129)

Food (fruit and veg)

Fruit

apples	jabłka	**jap**-ka
apricots	morele	mo-**re**-le
bananas	banany	ba-**na**-ni
cherries	czereśnie	che-**resh**-nye
grapefruit	grejpfrut	**greyp**-froot
grapes	winogrona	vee-no-**gro**-na
lemon	cytryna	tsit-**ri**-na
melon	melon	**me**-lon
oranges	pomarańcze	po-ma-**ran**-che
peaches	brzoskwinie	bzhos-**kfee**-nye
pears	gruszki	**groosh**-kee
plums	śliwki	**shleef**-kee
raspberries	maliny	ma-**lee**-ni
strawberries	truskawki	troos-**kaf**-kee
watermelon	arbuz	**ar**-boos

Vegetables

asparagus	**szparagi**	shpa-**ra**-gee
aubergine	**oberżyna**	o-ber-**zhi**-na
carrots	**marchew**	**mar**-hef
cauliflower	**kalafior**	ka-**la**-fyor
celery	**seler**	**se**-ler
courgettes	**cukinia**	tsoo-**kee**-nya
cucumber	**ogórek**	o-**goo**-rek
garlic	**czosnek**	**chos**-nek
leeks	**pory**	**po**-ri
lettuce	**sałata**	sa-**wa**-ta
mushrooms	**grzyby**	**gzhi**-bi
onions	**cebula**	tse-**boo**-la
peas	**groch**	groh
pepper	**papryka**	**pa**-pri-ka
potatoes	**ziemniaki**	zhem-**nya**-kee
runner beans	**fasola**	fa-**so**-la
salad	**sałatka**	sa-**wat**-ka
spinach	**szpinak**	**shpee**-nak
tomatoes	**pomidory**	po-mee-**do**-ri

Clothes

women's sizes		men's suit sizes		shoe sizes			
UK	EU	UK	EU	UK	EU	UK	EU
8	36	36	46	2	35	7	41
10	38	38	48	3	36	8	42
12	40	40	50	4	37	9	43
14	42	42	52	5	38	10	44
16	44	44	54	6	39	11	45
18	46	46	56				

May I try this on? **Czy mogę przymierzyć?**
chi **mo**-ge pshi-**mye**-zhich?

Do you have a small/medium/large size? **Czi jest mały/średni/duży/rozmiar?**
chi yest **ma**-wi/**shred**-nee/**doo**-zhi/**roz**-myar?

bigger **większy**
vyen-kshi

smaller **mniejszy**
mnyey-shi

in other colours **w innym kolorze**
v een-nim ko-**lo**-zhe

YOU MAY HEAR...	
Jaki numer buta ma pan/pani? **ya**-kee **noo**-mer **boo**-ta ma pan/**pa**-nee?	What shoe size do you take?
W tym kolorze jest tylko ten rozmiar f tim ko-**lo**-zhe yest **til**-ko ten **roz**-myar	In this colour we only have this size
Przymierzalnia jest tutaj pshi-mye-**zhal**-nya yest **too**-tay	The fitting room is there
Jaki jest pana/pani rozmiar? **ya**-kee yest **pa**-na/**pa**-nee **roz**-myar?	What size (clothes) do you wear?

Clothes (articles)

blouse	**bluzka**	**bloo**s-ka
coat	**kurtka**	**koor**-tka
dress (more formal)	**suknia/ sukienka**	**sook**-nya/ soo-**kyen**-ka

> **Paying** (p106) > **Numbers** (p 132)

jacket	**żakiet**	**zha**-kyet
jumper	**sweter**	**sfe**-ter
pants	**majtki**	**may**-tkee
shirt	**koszula**	ko-**shoo**-la
shorts	**szorty**	**shor**-ti
skirt	**spódnica**	spood-**nee**-tsa
socks	**skarpety**	skar-**pe**-ti
swimsuit	**kostium kąpielowy**	**kos**-tyoom kom-pye-**lo**-vi
t-shirt	**koszulka, ti shert**	ko-**shool**-ka
trousers	**spodnie**	**spod**-nye

Maps and guides

kiosk kyosk	kiosk
tygodnik ti-**god**-neek	a weekly magazine
gazeta ga-**ze**-ta	newspaper

Do you have a map...?	**Czy jest mapa...?** chi yest **ma**-pa...?
of the town	**miasta** **mya**-sta

> **Paying** (p 106)

of the region	**regionu** re-**gyo**-noo
Can you show me where ... is on the map?	**Czy może mi pan/pani pokazać na mapie?** chi **mo**-zhe mee pan/**pa**-nee po-**ka**-zach na **ma**-pye?
Do you have a guidebook/ a leaflet in English?	**Czy jest przewodnik/ broszura po angelsku?** chi yest pshe-**vod**-neek bro-**shoo**-ra po an-**gyel**-skoo?
Do you have any English newspapers/ books?	**Czy są angielskie gazety/ książki?** chi sow an-**gyel**-skye ga-**ze**-ti/ **kshon**-shkee?

Post office

A post office (**Poczta Polska**) provides the usual services and in some of them you can also buy bus/tram tickets. In big cities one post office (**Poczta Główna**) is open 24 hours and all others are open from 8.00 am until late afternoon.

> **Asking the way** (p 29) > **Sightseeing**(p 82)

poczta **poch**-ta	post office
znaczki **znach**-kee	stamps
paczki **pach**-kee	parcels
listy **lees**-ti	letters
lotnicza lot-**nee**-cha	airmail
lądowa lon-**do**-va	overland
ekspresem eks-**pre**-sem	special delivery
pocztą poleconą **poch**-tow po-le-**tso**-now	registered mail

Where is the post office?	Przepraszam, gdzie jest poczta? pshe-**pra**-sham, gdje yest **poch**-ta?
Which is the counter...?	W którym okienku są...? **f ktoo**-rim o-**kyen**-koo sow...?
for stamps	znaczki **znach**-kee
for parcels	paczki **pach**-kee
6 stamps for postcards...	sześć znaczków na pocztówki... shechch **znach**-koof na poch-**toof**-kee...

airmail	**lotniczą** lot-**nee**-chow
to Britain	**do Wielkiej Brytanii** do **vyel**-kyey bri-**tan**-ee
to America	**do Ameryki** do a-**me**-ri-kee
to Australia	**do Australii** do a-us-**tra**-lee

YOU MAY HEAR...

Znaczki można kupić w kiosku **znach**-kee **mozh**-na **koo**-peech **f kyos**-koo	You can buy stamps at the kiosk

> **Money** (p 104) > **Paying** (p 106)

Photos

Film can be bought at photographic shops, gift shops or supermarkets, but not at **apteka** (pharmacies).

A film for this camera	**Film do aparatu** feelm do a-pa-**ra**-too
Do you have batteries for this camera?	**Czy są baterie do tego aparatu?** chi sow ba-**te**-rye do **te**-go a-pa-**ra**-too?

Leisure

Sightseeing and tourist office

The tourist office is officially called Informacja Turystyczna. If you are looking for somewhere to stay, they will have details of hotels, campsites, etc. Tourist information can also be obtained from Orbis or PTTK (the Polish Tourist Organization).

Where is the tourist office?	Gdzie jest informacja turystyczna? gdje yest in-for-**ma**-tsya too-ris-**tich**-na?
What can we visit in the area?	Co można zobaczyć w okolicy? tso **mozh**-na zo-**ba**-chich v o-ko-**lee**-tsi?
in two hours?	przez dwie godziny? pshez dvye go-**djee**-ni?
Have you any leaflets?	Czy są jakieś broszury? chi sow **ya**-kyesh bro-**shoo**-ri?

Are there any excursions?	**Czy są jakieś wycieczki?** chi sow **ya**-kyesh vi-**chech**-kee?
We'd like to go to...	**Chcielibyśmy pojechać do...** **hche**-lee-bish-mi po-**ye**-hach do...
How much does it cost to get in?	**Ile kosztuje wstęp?** **ee**-le kosh-**too**-ye fstemp?
Are there reductions for...?	**Czy jest zniżka dla...?** chi yest **zneesh**-ka dla...?
children	**dzieci** **dje**-chee
students	**studentów** stoo-**den**-toof
over 60s	**emerytów** e-me-**ri**-toof

Entertainment

What is there to do in the evenings?	**Co można robić wieczorem?** tso **mozh**-na **ro**-beech vye-**cho**-rem?

Do you have a programme of events?	**Czy jest program imprez?** chi yest **pro**-gram **eem**-pres?
Is there anything for children?	**Czy są atrakcje dla dzieci?** chi sow a-**trak**-tsye dla **dje**-chee?

Leisure/interests

Where can I/ we go...?	**Gdzie można iść...?** gdje **mozh**-na eeshch...?
fishing	**na ryby** na **ri**-bi
walking	**na wycieczkę pieszą** na vi-**chech**-ke **pye**-show
Are there any good beaches near here?	**Czy jest tu dobra plaża?** chi yest too **do**-bra **pla**-zha?
Is there a swimming pool?	**Czy jest tu basen/ pływalnia?** chi yest too **ba**-sen/pwi-**val**-nya?

Music

Are there any good concerts on?	**Czy są jakieś dobre koncerty?** chi sow **ya**-kyesh **do**-bre kon-**tser**-ti?
Where can I get tickets for the concert?	**Gdzie mogę kupić bilety na koncert?** gdje **mo**-ge **koo**-peech bee-l**e**-ti na **kon**-tsert?
Where can we hear some classical music/jazz?	**Gdzie można posłuchać muzyki klasycznej/jazzu?** gdje **mozh**-na pos-**woo**-hach **moo**-zi-kee kla-**sich**-ney/ **dje**-zoo?

Cinema

What's on at the cinema (name of cinema) ...?	**Co grają w kinie...?** tso **gra**-yow **f kee**-nye...?

> **Making friends** (p 22)

What time does the film start?	**O której zaczyna się film?** o **ktoo**-rey za-**chi**-na she feelm?
How much are the tickets?	**Ile kosztują bilety?** **ee**-le kosh-**too**-yow bee-**le**-ti?
Two for the... (give time of performance) showing	**dwa na godzinę...** dva na go-**djee**-ne...

Theatre/opera

parter **par**-ter	stalls
galeria ga-**ler**-ya	circle
galeria na górze ga-**ler**-ya na **goo**-zhe	upper circle
loża **lo**-zha	box
miejsce **myey**-stse	seat
garderoba/szatnia gar-de-**ro**-ba/**shat**-nya	cloakroom

What's on at the theatre?	**Co grają w teatrze?** tso **gra**-yow f te-**at**-she?
How much are the tickets?	**Ile kosztują bilety?** **ee**-le kosh-**too**-yow bee-**le**-ti?

I'd like two tickets...	**Proszę dwa bilety...** **pro**-she dva bee-**le**-ti...
for tonight	**na dziś wieczór** na djeesh **vye**-choor
for tomorrow night	**na jutro wieczór** na **yoo**-tro **vye**-choor
for the 3rd of August	**na 3-ego sierpnia** na tshe-**che**-go **sher**-pnya
When does the performance begin/end?	**O której zaczyna się przedstawienie?** o **ktoo**-rey za-**chi**-na she pshet-sta-**vye**-nye?

YOU MAY HEAR...

Nie można wejść, przedstawienie zaczęło się nye **mozh**-na **vey**shch, pshet-sta-**vye**-nye za-**che**-wo she	You can't go in, the performance has started
Można wejść podczas przerwy **mozh**-na veyshch **pot**-chas **psher**-vi	You may enter at the interval

Television

pilot **pee**-lot	remote control
włączyć **vwon**-chich	to switch on
wyłączyć vi-**won**-chich	to switch off
serial **ser**-yal	series
telenowela te-le-no-**ve**-la	soap
wiadomości vya-do-**mosh**-cheee	news
filmy animowane **feel**-mi a-nee-mo-**va**-ne	cartoons

Where is the television? **Gdzie jest telewizor?**
gdje yest te-le-**vee**-zor?

How do you switch it on? **Jak się go włącza?**
yak she go **vwon**-cha?

What's on television? **Co jest w telewizji?**
tso yest f tele-**vee**-zee?

When is the news on? **Kiedy są wiadomości?**
kye-di sow vya-do-**mosh**-chee?

Do you have any English-language channels? **Czy są angielskie kanały?**
chi sow an-**gyels**-kye ka-**na**-wi?

Do you have any English videos? **Czy są angielskie taśmy video?**
chi sow an-**gyels**-kye **tash**-mi vee-**de**-o?

Sport

The most popular sport is football, but aside from this there are plenty of opportunities for other outdoor pursuits such as hiking, mountain climbing, fishing, swimming, sailing, horse riding, skiing and hunting.

Where can we play...? **Gdzie można grać w...?**
gdje **mozh**-na grach f...?

Where can I/ we go...? **Gdzie można...?**
gdje **mozh**-na...?

swimming **pływać**
pwi-vach

jogging **biegać**
bye-gach

Do you have to be a member? **Czy trzeba być członkiem?**
chi **tshe**-ba bich **chwon**-kyem?

Sport

How much is it per hour?	Ile kosztuje od godziny? **ee**-le kosh-**too**-ye od go-**djee**-ni?
Can we hire...?	Czy można wynająć...? chi **mozh**-na vi-**na**-yonch...?
rackets	rakiety ra-**kye**-ti
golf clubs	kije golfowe **kee**-ye gol-**fo**-ve
We'd like to see (name team) play	Chcielibyśmy zobaczyć grę... **hche**-lee-bish-mi zo-**ba**-chich gre...
Where can I/we get tickets for (name of game)...?	Gdzie można dostać bilety na...? gdje **mozh**-na **dos**-tach bee-**le**-ti na to...?

YOU MAY HEAR...

Nie ma już biletów nye ma yoosh bee-**le**-toof	There are no tickets left for the game

Skiing

narty biegowe **nar**-ti bye-**go**-ve	cross-country skiing
karnet na wyciąg **kar**-net na **vi**-chonk	ski pass
wyciąg **vi**-chonk	chair lift

Can I/we hire skis?	**Czy można wynająć narty?** chi **mozh**-na vi-**na**-yonch **nar**-ti?
Does the price include...?	**Czy w tej cenie są...?** chi v tey **tse**-nye sow...?
boots	**buty** **boo**-ti
poles	**kijki** **keey**-kee
How much is a ... pass?	**Ile kosztuje karnet na wyciąg...?** **ee**-le kosh-**too**-ye **kar**-net na **vi**-chonk...?
daily	**na dzień** na djen
weekly	**na tydzień** na **ti**-djen

When is the last ascent? — **Kiedy jest ostatni wjazd?**
kye-di yest os-**tat**-nee vyast?

Can you tighten my bindings? — **Czy może mi pan/pani zacisnąć wiązadła?**
chi **mo**-zhe mee pan/**pa**-nee za-**chees**-nonch vyon-**zad**-wa?

YOU MAY HEAR...	
Czy umie pan/pani jeździć na nartach? chi **oo**-mye pan/**pa**-nee **yezh**-djeech na **nar**-tach?	Can you ski at all?
Jaki jest pana/pani numer buta? **ya**-kee yest **pa**-na/**pa**-nee **noo**-mer **boo**-ta?	What is your boot size?
Czy chce pan/pani brać lekcje jazdy na nartach? chi htse pan/**pa**-nee brach **lek**-tsye **yaz**-di na **nar**-tah?	Do you want skiing lessons?

Walking

Are there any guided walks?	**Czy są wycieczki piesze z przewodnikiem?** chi sow vi-**chech**-kee **pye**-she s pshe-vod-**nee**-kyem?
Do you know of any good walks?	**Czy można tu robić dobre wycieczki piesze?** chi **mozh**-na too **ro**-beech **dob**-re vi-**chech**-kee **pye**-she?
How many kilometres is the walk?	**Ile to jest kilometrów?** **ee**-le to yest kee-lo-**met**-roof?
Is it very steep?	**Czy jest bardzo stromo?** chi yest **bar**-djo **stro**-mo?
How long will it take?	**Ile czasu zabierze ta wycieczka?** **ee**-le **cha**-soo za-**bye**-zhe ta vi-**chech**-ka?
Is there a map of the walk?	**Czy jest mapa tego szlaku?** chi yest **ma**-pa **te**-go **shla**-koo?
We'd like to go climbing	**Chcielibyśmy pójść na wspinaczkę** **hche**-lee-bish-my pooyshch na fspee-**nach**-ke

Do you have a detailed map of the area?	**Czy jest szczegółowa mapa terenu?** chi yest shche-goo-**wo**-va **ma**-pa te-**re**-noo?

> **Maps and guides** (p 77)

Communications

Telephone and mobile

The international code for Poland is **0048** plus the Polish town or area code less the first **0**, for example, Warsaw **(0)22**, Poznań **(0)61**, Kraków **(0)12**.

karta telefoniczna **kar**-ta te-le-fo-**neech**-na	phonecard
telefon komórkowy/ komórka te-**le**-fon ko-moor-**ko**-vi/ ko-**moor**-ka	mobile

I want to make a phone call — **Czy mogę zatelefonować?**
chi **mo**-ge za-te-le-fo-**no**-vach?

Where can I buy a phonecard? — **Gdzie mogę kupić kartę telefoniczną?**
gdje **mo**-ge **koo**-pich **kar**-te te-le-fo-**neech**-now?

A phonecard for ... zloties	**Proszę kartę telefoniczną za ... złotych** **pro**-she **kar**-te te-le-fo-**neech**-now za ... **zwo**-tich
Have you got a mobile phone?	**Czy ma pan/pani komórkę?** chi ma pan/**pa**-nee ko-**moor**-ke?
What is your mobile phone number?	**Jaki jest numer pana/pani komórki?** **ya**-kee yest **noo**-mer **pa**-na/**pa**-nee ko-**moor**-kee?
My mobile number is...	**Numer mojej komórki to...** **noo**-mer **mo**-yey ko-**moor**-kee to...
What's the extension number?	**Jaki jest numer wewnętrzny?** **ya**-kee yest **noo**-mer vev-**nen**-tshni?

FACE TO FACE

A **Słucham**
swoo-ham
Hello

B **Chciałbym/chciałabym rozmawiać z...**
hchaw-bim/**hcha**-wa-bim roz-**ma**-vyach z...
I'd like to speak to ..., please

A **Kto mówi?**
kto **moo**-vee?
Who's calling?

B **Mówi David**
moo-vee **da**-veet
It's David

A **Chwileczkę...**
hvee-**lech**-ke...
Just a moment...

Can I speak to...?	**Czy mogę rozmawiać z...?** chi **mo**-ge roz-**ma**-vyach z...?
I'll call back later	**Zadzwonię później** za-**dzvo**-nye **poozh**-nyey
I'll call back tomorrow	**Zadzwonię jutro** za-**dzvo**-nye **yoo**-tro
This is... (followed by the name of the person speaking)	**Mówi...** **moo**-vee...
How do I get an outside line?	**Jak wybrać zewnętrzną linię?** yak **vi**-brach zev-**nen**-tshnow **lee**-nye?

YOU MAY HEAR...	
Próbuję połączyć proo-**boo**-ye po-**won**-chich	I'm trying to connect you
Linia jest zajęta. Proszę spróbować później **lee**-nya yest za-**yen**-ta **pro**-she sproo-**bo**-vach **poozh**-nyey	The line is engaged. Please try later
Czy chce pan/pani zostawić wiadomość? chi htse pan/**pa**-nee zos-**ta**-veech vya-**do**-moshch?	Do you want to leave a message?
...proszę zostawić wiadomość po sygnale ...**pro**-she zos-**ta**-veech vya-**do**-moshch po sig-**na**-le	...please leave a message after the tone
Proszę wyłączyć wszystkie telefony komórkowe **pro**-she vi-**won**-chich **fshis**-tkye te-le-**fo**-ni ko-moor-**ko**-ve	Please switch off all mobile phones

Text messaging

SMS is widely used in Poland.

I will text you (informal)	**Wyślę ci esemesa** **vi**-shle chee es-em-**es**-a
Can you text me?	**Czy możesz mi wysłać esemesa?** chi **mo**-zhesh mee **vis**-wach es-em-**es**-a?

E-mail

An informal way of writing an email is to address it with **Cześć...!** (Hi/Hello) and end it with **Na razie** (bye for now). For more formal e-mails, begin with either **Szanowny Panie** (for a man) or **Szanowna Pani** (for a woman).

New message	**Nowa wiadomość**
To	**Do**
From	**Od**
Subject	**Temat**
Cc	**Cc**
Bcc	**Ccn**
Attachment	**Załącznik**
Send	**Wyślij**

Do you have an e-mail?	**Czy ma pan/pani e-mail?** chi ma pan/**pa**-nee e-mail?
What is your e-mail address?	**Jaki jest pana/pani adres mailowy?** **ya**-kee yest **pa**-na/**pa**-nee **ad**-res mai-**lo**-vi?
How do you spell it?	**Jak to się pisze?** yak to she **pee**-she?
All one word	**Jedno słowo** **yed**-no **swo**-vo
All lower case	**Małe litery** **ma**-we lee-**te**-ri
My e-mail address is...	**Mój adres mailowy to...** mooy **ad**-res mei-**lo**-vi to...

clare.smith@ bit.co.uk	**clare kropka smith małpa bit kropka co kropka uk** klare **krop**-ka smith **maw**-pa bit **krop**-ka ko **krop**-ka oo ka
Can I send an e-mail?	**Czy mogę wysłać e-mail?** chi **mo**-ge **vi**-swach e-mail?
Did you get my e-mail?	**Czy doszedł mój e-mail?** chi **do**-shed mooy e-mail?

Internet

Computer terminology tends to be in English and you will find the same with the internet.

Are there any internet cafés here?	**Czy jest tu kawiarenka internetowa?** chi yest too ka-vya-**re**-nka een-ter-ne-**to**-va?
How much is it to log on for an hour?	**Ile kosztuje godzina na internecie?** **ee**-le kosh-**too**-ye go-**djee**-na na een-ter-**ne**-che?

Fax

The code to send faxes to Poland from Britain is **0048** plus the Polish area code without the first **0**, for example, Warsaw **0048 22,** Kraków **0048 12**.

Addressing a fax

do	to
od	from
data	date
temat:	re:
tekst	text/body of the fax
...**stron/strony**	...pages in total

Do you have a fax?	**Czy jest tu faks?** chi yest too fax?
I want to send a fax	**Chciałbym/chciałabym wysłać faks** **hchaw**-bim/**hcha**-wa-bim **vis**-wach fax

Communications

What is your fax number?	**Jaki jest numer pana/pani faksu?** **ya**-kee yest **noo**-mer **pa**-na/ **pa**-nee **fa**-xoo?
My fax number is...	**Numer mojego faksu...** **noo**-mer mo-**ye**-go **fa**-xoo...

Practicalities

Money

Banks are usually open from 8.00 am to 6.00 pm on weekdays. The currency is Polish złoty and grosz (pence). There are numerous currency exchange offices, kantor, which tend to have a better exchange rate than banks.

Karta kredytowa **ka**-rta kre-di-**to**-va	credit card
Bankomat ban-**ko**-mat	cash machine (ATM)
Kwit kfeet	till receipt

Where can I change some money? — Gdzie mogę wymienić pieniądze?
gdje **mo**-ge vi-**mye**-neech pye-**nyon**-dze?

When does the bank open? — O której otwiera się bank?
o **ktoo**-rey ot-**fye**-ra she bank?

When does the bank close?	O której zamyka się bank? o **ktoo**-rey za-**mi**-ka she bank?
Can I pay with...?	Czy mogę zapłacić w...? chi **mo**-ge za-**pwa**-cheech v...?
euros	euro **eu**-ro
English pounds	w angielskich funtach an-**gyel**-skeeh **foon**-tah
I want to change these travellers cheques	Czy mogę zrealizować czeki podróżne? chi **mo**-ge zre-a-lee-**zo**-vach **che**-kee pod-**roozh**-ne?
Where is the nearest cash machine?	Gdzie jest najbliższy bankomat? gdje yest nay-**bleesh**-shi ban-**ko**-mat?
Can I use my credit card at the cash machine?	Czy mogę użyć karty kredytowej w bankomacie? chi m**o**-ge **oo**-zhich **kar**-ti kre-di-**to**-vey v ban-ko-**ma**-che?
Do you have any loose change?	Czy ma pan/pani drobne? chi ma pan/**pa**-nee **drob**-ne?

Paying

How much is it?	Ile to kosztuje? **ee**-le to kosh-**too**-ye?
How much will it be?	Ile to będzie? **ee**-le to **ben**-dje?
Can I pay by...?	Czy mogę zapłacić...? chi **mo**-ge za-**pwa**-cheech...?
credit card	kartą kredytową **kar**-tow kre-di-**to**-vow
cheque	czekiem **che**-kyem
Is service included?	Czy to razem z obsługą? chi to **ra**-zem z op-**swoo**-gow?
I need a receipt, please	Proszę o pokwitowanie/ paragon **pro**-she o po-kfee-to-**va**-nye/ pa-**ra**-gon
Do I pay in advance?	Czy muszę zapłacić z góry? chi **moo**-she za-**pwa**-cheech **z goo**-ri?
Do I need to pay a deposit?	Czy muszę dać depozyt? chi **moo**-she dach de-**po**-zit?
I'm sorry	Przepraszam pshe-**pra**-sham

I've nothing smaller (no change)	nie mam drobnych nye mam **drob**-nih

YOU MAY HEAR...

Obsługa jest wliczona, ale bez napiwku op-**swoo**-ga yest vlee-**cho**-na, ale bez na-**peef**-koo	Service is included but not a tip
Zapłata przy kasie za-**pwa**-ta pshi **ka**-she	Pay at the till
Proszę najpierw otrzymać paragon w kasie **pro**-she **nay**-pyerv o-**tshi**-mach pa-**ra**-gon **f ka**-she	First get a receipt at the till (at airport, station bars, etc.)

Luggage

odbiór bagażu **od**-byoor ba-**ga**-zhoo	baggage reclaim
przechowalnia bagażu pshe-ho-**val**-nya ba-**ga**-zhoo	left-luggage office
wózek bagażowy **voo**-zek ba-ga-**zho**-vi	luggage trolley

My luggage hasn't arrived — Nie ma mojego bagażu
nye ma mo-**ye**-go ba-**ga**-zhoo

My suitcase has been damaged — Moja walizka jest uszkodzona
mo-ya vą-**lees**-ka yest oosh-ko-**dzo**-na

> **Train** (p 37) > **Air travel** (p45)

Repairs

This is broken	To jest zepsute to yest zep-**soo**-te
Where can I have this repaired?	Gdzie można to zreperować? gdje **mozh**-na to zre-pe-**ro**-vach?
Is it worth repairing?	Czy warto to zreperować? chi **var**-to to zre-pe-**ro**-vach?
Can you repair...?	Czy można zreperować...? chi **mozh**-na zre-pe-**ro**-vach...?
this	to to
these shoes	te buty te **boo**-ti
my watch	mój zegarek mooy ze-**ga**-rek

YOU MAY HEAR...

Niestety nie możemy tego zreperować nyes-**te**-ti nye mo-**zhe**-mi **te**-go zre-pe-**ro**-vach	Sorry, but we can't mend it

> **Breakdown** (p 54)

Laundry

pralnia chemiczna/ sucha pralnia **pral**-nya he-**meech**-na/ **soo**-ha **pral**-nya	dry-cleaner's
proszek do prania **pro**-shek do **pra**-nya	soap powder
wybielacz vi-**bye**-lach	bleach
pralka **pral**-ka	washing machine
suszarka soo-**shar**-ka	tumble dryer

Where can I wash these clothes? Gdzie mogę zrobić pranie?
gdje **mo**-ge **zro**-beech **pra**-nye?

Where is the nearest launderette? Gdzie jest najbliższa pralnia?
gdje yest nay-**bleesh**-sha **pral**-nya?

Practicalities

Complaints

This does not work	To nie działa to nye **dja**-wa
It's dirty	To jest brudne to yest **brood**-ne
light	światło **shfyat**-wo
toilet	toaleta to-a-**le**-ta
heating	ogrzewanie og-zhe-**va**-nye
air conditioning	klimatyzycja klee-ma-ti-**za**-tsya
It's broken	To jest zepsute to yest zep-**soo**-te
I want a refund	Proszę o zwrot pieniędzy **pro**-she o zvrot pye-**nyen**-dzi

> **Hotel (booking)** (p 60)

Problems

Can you help me?	Czy mogę prosić o pomoc? chi **mo**-ge **pro**-sheech o **po**-mots?
I don't speak Polish	Nie mówię po polsku nye **moo**-vye po **pol**-skoo
Does anyone here speak English?	Czy ktoś tu mówi po angielsku? chi ktosh too **moo**-vee po an-**gyel**-skoo?
What's the matter?	O co chodzi? o tso **ho**-djee?
I would like to speak to whoever is in charge of...	Chciałbym/chciałabym mówić z kierownikiem **hchaw**-bim/**hcha**-wa-bim **moo**-veech s kye-rov-**nee**-kyem
I'm lost	Zgubiłem(łam) się zgoo-**bee**-wem(wam) she
How do you get to...? (on foot)	Jak dojść do...? yak doyshch do..?

I missed my train/plane/ connection	Spóźniłem(łam) się na pociąg/na samolot/ na połączenie spoozh-**nee**-wem(wam) she na **po**-chonk/na sa-**mo**-lot/ na po-won-**che**-nye
I've missed my flight because there was a strike	Spóźniłem(łam) się na samolot bo był strajk spoozh-**nee**-wem(wam) she na sa-**mo**-lot bo biw strayk
The coach has left without me	Autokar odjechał beze mnie au-**to**-kar od-**ye**-how be-**zem**-nye
Can you show me how this works, please?	Czy może mi pan/pani pokazać jak to działa? chi **mo**-zhe mee pan/**pa**-nee po-**ka**-zach yak to **dja**-wa?
I have lost my money	Zgubiłem(łam) pieniądze zgoo-**bee**-wem(wam) pye-**nyon**-dze
I need to get to (on foot) ...	Muszę iść do... **moo**-she eeshch do...

Problems

I need to get in touch with the British consulate	Muszę skontaktować się z Konsulatem Brytyjskim **moo**-she skon-tak-**to**-vach she s kon-soo-**la**-tem bri-**tiys**-keem
Please leave me alone!	Proszę zostawić mnie w spokoju! **pro**-she zos-**ta**-veech mnye f spo-**ko**-yoo!

Emergencies

pogotowie ratunkowe po-go-**to**-vye ra-toon-**ko**-ve	ambulance
policja po-**lee**-tsya	police
straż pożarna strash po-**zhar**-na	fire brigade
strażak **stra**-zhak	fireman
komisariat policji ko-mee-**sa**-ryat po-**lee**-tsee	police station

Help!	Pomocy! po-**mo**-tsi!
Fire!	Pożar! **po**-zhar!

Can you help me?	Proszę o pomoc? **pro**-she o **po**-mots?
There's been an accident!	Jest wypadek! yest vi-**pa**-dek!
Someone...	Ktoś... ktosh...
has been injured	jest ranny yest **ran**-ni
has been knocked down	został przewrócony **zo**-staw pshe-vroo-**tso**-ni
Please call...	Proszę zawołać... **pro**-she za-**vo**-wach...
the police	policję po-**lee**-tsye
an ambulance	pogotowie po-go-**to**-vye
Where is the police station?	Gdzie jest komisariat policji? gdje yest ko-mee-**sar**-yat po-**lee**-tsee?
I want to report a crime	Chcę zgłosić przestępstwo htse **zgwo**-sheech pshes-**tem**-pstfo
I've been robbed	Okradziono mnie o-kra-**djo**-no mnye

I've been attacked	Napadnięto mnie na-pad-**nyen**-to mnye
Someone's stolen...	Ukradli mi... ook-**rad**-lee mee...
my bag	torbę **tor**-be
traveller's cheques	czeki podróżne **che**-kee pod-**roozh**-ne
My car has been broken into	Ktoś włamał się do mojego samochodu ktosh **vwa**-maw she do mo-**ye**-go sa-mo-**ho**-doo
My car has been stolen	Ukradziono mi samochód ook-ra-**djo**-no mee sa-**mo**-hoot
I've been raped	Zostałam zgwałcona zos-**ta**-wam zgvaw-**tso**-na
I want to speak to a policewoman	Chcę rozmawiać z policjantką htse roz-**ma**-vyach s po-lee-**tsyant**-kow
I need to make a telephone call	Muszę zadzwonić **moo**-she za-**dzvo**-neech

Practicalities

I need a report for my insurance	Potrzebuję raport dla firmy ubezpieczeniowej po-tshe-**boo**-ye **ra**-port dla **feer**-mi oo-bes-pye-che-**nyo**-vey
I didn't know there was a speed limit	Nie wiedziałem(łam) że jest ograniczenie prędkości nye vye-**dja**-wem(wam) zhe yest o-gra-nee-**che**-nye prent-**kosh**-chee
How much is the fine?	Ile wynosi mandat? **ee**-le vi-**no**-shee **man**-dat?
Where do I pay it?	Gdzie płacę? gdje **pwa**-tse?
Do I have to pay it straightaway?	Czy muszę zapłacić od razu? chi **moo**-she za-**pwa**-cheech od-**ra**-zoo?
I'm very sorry	Bardzo przepraszam **bar**-dzo pshe-**pra**-sham

Health

Pharmacy

apteka ap-**te**-ka	pharmacy/chemist
dyżurny aptekarz di-**zhoor**-ni ap-**te**-kash	duty chemist

Can you give me something for...?	**Czy mogę dostać coś na...?** chi **mo**-ge **dos**-tach tsosh na...?
a headache	**ból głowy** bool **gwo**-vi
car sickness	**chorobę lokomocyjną** ho-**ro**-be lo-ko-mo-**tsiy**-now
a cough	**kaszel** **ka**-shel
diarrhoea	**rozwolnienie** roz-vol-**nye**-nye
Is it safe for children?	**Czy to bezpieczne dla dzieci?** chi to bes-**pyech**-ne dla **dje**-chee?

How much should I give him/her?	**Ile mogę mu/jej dać?** **ee**-le **mo**-ge moo/yey dach?

YOU MAY HEAR...

Trzy razy dziennie przed/po jedzeniu tshi **ra**-zi **djen**-nye pshet/ po ye-**dzen**-yoo	Three times a day before/after meals

Doctor

szpital **shpee**-tal	hospital
nagły wypadek **nag**-wi vi-**pa**-dek	casualty
przychodnia lekarska pshi-**hod**-nya le-**kars**-ka	local health centre

FACE TO FACE

A **Źle się czuję**
zhle she **choo**-ye
I feel ill

B **Czy ma pan/pani temperaturę?**
chi ma pan/**pa**-nee tem-pe-ra-**too**-re?
Do you have a temperature?

A **Nie. Boli mnie tu...**
nye, **bo**-lee mnye too...
No, I feel pain here...

I need a doctor	**Potrzebuję lekarza** po-tshe-**boo**-ye le-**ka**-zha
My son is ill	**Mój syn jest chory** moy sin yest **ho**-ri
My daughter is ill	**Moja córka jest chora** **mo**-ya **tsoor**-ka yest **ho**-ra
I'm diabetic	**Mam cukrzycę** mam tsook-**shi**-tse
I'm pregnant	**Jestem w ciąży** yes-tem **f chon**-zhi
I'm on the pill	**Jestem na tabletkach antykoncepcyjnych** yes-tem na tab-**let**-kah an-ti-kon-tsep-**tsiy**-nih

I'm allergic to penicillin (m/f)	**Jestem uczulony(a) na penicylinę** **yes**-tem oo-choo-**lo**-ni(a) na pe-nee-tsi-**lee**-ne
Will he/she have to go to hospital?	**Czy on/ona musi iść do szpitala?** chi on/ona **moo**-shee eeshch do shpee-**ta**-la?
When are the visiting hours?	**Kiedy są godziny odwiedzin?** **kye**-di sow go-**djee**-ni od-**vye**-djeen?
Will I have to pay?	**Czy muszę zapłacić?** chi **moo**-she zap-**wa**-cheech?
How much will it cost?	**Ile to będzie kosztować?** **ee**-le to **ben**-dje kosh-**to**-vach?
Can you give me a receipt for the insurance?	**Czy mogę dostać kwit dla firmy ubezpieczeniowej?** chi **mo**-ge **dos**-tach kfeet dla **fee**-rmi oo-bes-pye-che-**nyo**-vey?

YOU MAY HEAR...

Musi pan/pani iść do szpitala **moo**-shee pan/**pa**-nee eeshch do shpee-**ta**-la	You will have to go to hospital
To nic poważnego to neets po-wazh-**ne**-go	It's not serious

Dentist

I need a dentist	**Potrzebuję dentysty** po-tshe-**boo**-ye den-**tis**-ti
He/she has toothache	**Boli go/ją ząb** **bo**-lee go/yow zomp
Can you do a temporary filling?	**Czy można zrobić tymczasową plombę?** chi **mozh**-na **zro**-beech tim-cha-**so**-vow **plom**-be?
It hurts	**Boli** **bo**-lee

Health

> **Emergencies** (p114)

Can you give me something for the pain?	**Czy mogę dostać coś na ból?** chi **mo**-ge **dos**-tach tsosh na bool?
Can you repair my dentures?	**Czy można zreperować moją protezę?** chi **mozh**-na zre-pe-**ro**-vach **mo**-yow pro-**te**-ze?
Do I have to pay?	**Czy muszę zapłacić?** chi **moo**-she za-**pwa**-cheech?
How much will it be?	**Ile to kosztuje?** **ee**-le to kosh-**too**-ye?
Can I have a receipt for my insurance?	**Proszę o rachunek dla ubezpieczalni** **pro**-she o ra-**hoo**-nek dla oo-bes-pye-**chal**-nee

YOU MAY HEAR...

Trzeba go wyrwać **tshe**-ba go **vir**-vach	I'll have to take it out
Trzeba to zaplombować **tshe**-ba to za-plom-**bo**-vach	You need a filling
To może trochę boleć to **mo**-zhe **tro**-he **bo**-lech	This might hurt a little

> **Pharmacy** (p 118)

Different types of travellers

Disabled travellers

What facilities do you have for disabled people?	Jakie są ułatwienia dla niepełnosprawnych? **ya**-kye sow oo-wat-**fye**-nya dla nye-pe-wno-**sprav**-nih?
Are there any toilets for the disabled?	Czy są toalety dla niepełnosprawnych? chi sow to-a-**le**-ti dla nye-pe-wno-**sprav**-nih?
Do you have any bedrooms on the ground floor?	Czy są pokoje na parterze? chi sow po-**ko**-ye na par-**te**-zhe?
Is there a lift?	Czy jest winda? chi yest **veen**-da?
Where is the lift?	Gdzie jest winda? gdje yest **veen**-da?
Can you visit ... in a wheelchair?	Czy można odwiedzić ... na wózku inwalidzkim? chi **mozh**-na od-**vye**-djeech ... na **voos**-koo een-va-**leets**-keem?

Do you have any wheelchairs?	Czy są wózki inwalidzkie? chi sow **voos**-kee een-va-**leets**-kye?
Where is the wheelchair-accessible entrance?	Gdzie można wjechać wózkiem inwalidzkim? gdje **mozh**-na **vye**-hach **voos**-kyem een-va-**leets**-keem?
Is there a reduction for disabled people?	Czy jest zniżka dla ludzi niepełnosprawnych? chi yest **zneesh**-ka dla **loo**-djee nye-pe-wno-**sprav**-nih?
Is there somewhere I can sit down?	Czy można tu gdzieś usiąść? chi **mozh**-na too gdjesh **oo**-shon-shch?

With kids

Public transport is free for children under 4. Children between the ages of 4 and 12 pay half price.

A child's ticket	Bilet dla dziecka **bee**-let dla **djets**-ka

> **Hotel (booking)** (p 60)

He/She is ... years old	on/ona ma ... lata/lat on/ona ma ... **la**-ta/lat
Is there a reduction for children?	Czy jest zniżka dla dzieci? chi yest **zneesh**-ka dla dje-chee?
Do you have a children's menu?	Czy jest karta dla dzieci? chi yest **kar**-ta dla **dje**-chee?
Is it OK to take children?	Czy można wziąść dzieci? chi **mozh**-na vzhonshch **dje**-chee?
Do you have...?	Czy macie ...? chi **ma**-che ...?
a high chair	wysokie krzesełko vi-**so**-kye kshe-**sew**-ko
a cot	łóżeczko woo-**zhech**-ko
I have two children	Mam dwoje dzieci mam **dvo**-ye **dje**-chee
Do you have any children?	Czy ma pan/pani dzieci? chi ma pan/**pa**-nee **dje**-chee?

> **Pharmacy** (p 118) > **Doctor** (p 119)

Reference

Alphabet

The letters X, V and Q do not exist in Polish. You will only see these letters in foreign words. Below are the words used for clarification when spelling something out.

Jak to się pisze? yak to she **pee**-she	How do you spell it?
A jak Anna, B jak Barbara a yak **an**-na b yak bar-**ba**-ra	A like Anna, B like Barbara

A	a	**Anna**	**an**-na
B	beh	**barka**	**bar**-ka
C	tseh	**cena**	**tse**-na
Ć	chee	**ćma**	chma
D	deh	**dom**	dom
E	eh	**Ewa**	**eh**-va
F	ef	**forma**	**for**-ma

G	gyeh	**gra**	gra
H	ha	**hotel**	**ho**-tel
I	ee	**inny**	**een**-ni
J	yot	**jama**	**ya**-ma
K	ka	**kasa**	**ka**-sa
L	el	**Litwa**	**leet**-fa
Ł	ehw	**Łódź**	wooch
M	em	**miasto**	**myas**-to
N	en	**nowa**	**no**-va
Ń	enh	**cień**	chenh
O	o	**ostry**	**os**-tri
Ó	oo	**ból**	bool
P	peh	**prosto**	**pros**-to
R	er	**rower**	**ro**-ver
S	es	**sowa**	**so**-va
Ś	esh	**śląsk**	shlonsk
T	teh	**tor**	tor
U	oo	**usta**	**oos**-ta
W	voo	**wino**	**vee**-no
Y	eegrek	**dym**	dim
Z	zet	**zorza**	**zo**-zha
Ż	zhet	**żona**	**zho**-na
Ź	zhet	**źle**	zhle

Measurements and quantities

1 lb = approx. 0.5 kilo   1 pint = approx. 0.5 litre

Liquids

1/2 litre of...	**pół litra** ... **poow leet**-ra...
a litre of...	**litr**... leetr...
1/2 a bottle of...	**pół butelki** poow boo-**tel**-kee
a bottle of...	**butelka**... boo-**tel**-ka...
a glass of... (for wine)	**kieliszek** kye-**lee**-shek
a glass of ... (for non-alcoholic drinks)	**szklanka** **shklan**-ka

Weights

100 grams	**100 gramów** sto **gra**-moof
1/2 a kilo of...	**pół kilo...** poow **kee**-lo
a kilo of...	**kilo...** **kee**-lo

Food

a slice of...	**kawałek...** ka-**va**-wek...
a portion of...	**porcja...** **por**-tsya...
a dozen...	**tuzin...** **too**-zheen...
a box of...	**pudełko...** poo-**dew**-ko...
a packet of...	**paczka...** **pach**-ka...
a tin of...	**puszka...** **poosh**-ka...
a jar of...	**słoik...** **swo**-eek...

Miscellaneous

...euro's worth of...	**za ... euro** za ... **eoo**-ro
a quarter	**ćwiartka** **chfyart**-ka
20 per cent	**dwadzieścia procent** dva-**djesh**-cha **pro**-tsent
more than...	**więcej niż...** **vyen**-tsey neesh...
less than...	**mniej niż...** **mnyey** neesh...
double	**podwójnie** pod-**vooy**-nye
twice	**dwa razy** dva **ra**-zi

Numbers

0 **zero ze**-ro
1 **jeden ye**-den
2 **dwa** dva
3 **trzy** tshi
4 **cztery chte**-ri
5 **pięć** pyench
6 **sześć** sheshch
7 **siedem she**-dem
8 **osiem o**-shem
9 **dziewięć dje**-vyench
10 **dziesięć dje**-shench
11 **jedenaście** ye-de-**nash**-che
12 **dwanaście** dva-**nash**-che
13 **trzynaście** tshi-**nash**-che
14 **czternaście** chter-**nash**-che
15 **piętnaście** pyet-**nash**-che
16 **szesnaście** shes-**nash**-che
17 **siedemnaście** she-dem-**nash**-che
18 **osiemnaście** o-shem-**nash**-che
19 **dziewiętnaście** dje-vyet-**nash**-che
20 **dwadzieścia** dva-**djesh**-cha
21 **dwadzieścia jeden**
dva-**djesh**-cha **ye**-den

Reference

22	**dwadzieścia dwa** dva-**djesh**-cha dva
23	**dwadzieścia trzy** dva-**djesh**-cha tshi
24	**dwadzieścia cztery** dva-**djesh**-cha **chte**-ri
25	**dwadzieścia pięć** dva-**djesh**-cha pyench
26	**dwadzieścia sześć** dva-**djesh**-cha sheshch
27	**dwadzieścia siedem** dva-**djesh**-cha **she**-dem
28	**dwadzieścia osiem** dva-**djesh**-cha **o**-shem
29	**dwadzieścia dziewięć** dva-**djesh**-cha **dje**-vyench
30	**trzydzieści** tshi-**djesh**-chee
40	**czterdzieści** chter-**djesh**-chee
50	**pięćdziesiąt** pyen-**dje**-shont
60	**sześćdziesiąt** shesh-**dje**-shont
70	**siedemdziesiąt** she-dem-**dje**-shont
80	**osiemdziesiąt** o-shem-**dje**-shont
90	**dziewięćdziesiąt** dje-vyen-**dje**-shont
100	**sto** sto
110	**sto dziesięć** sto **dje**-shench
1000	**tysiąc** **ti**-shonts
2000	**dwa tysiące** dva ti-**shon**-tse

1 million **milion** **meel**-yon
1 billion **miliard** **meel**-yard

1st	**pierwszy** **pyerf**-shi	6th	**szósty** **shoos**-ti
2nd	**drugi** **droo**-gee	7th	**siódmy** **shood**-mi
3rd	**trzeci** **tshe**-chee	8th	**ósmy** **oos**-mi
4th	**czwarty** **chfar**-ti	9th	**dziewiąty** dje-**vyon**-ti
5th	**piąty** **pyon**-ti	10th	**dziesiąty** dje-**shon**-ti

Days and months

Days

Monday	**poniedziałek**	po-nye-**dja**-wek
Tuesday	**wtorek**	**fto**-rek
Wednesday	**środa**	**shro**-da

Thursday	**czwartek**	**chfar**-tek
Friday	**piątek**	**pyon**-tek
Saturday	**sobota**	so-**bo**-ta
Sunday	**niedziela**	nye-**dje**-la

Months

January	**styczeń**	**st**i-chenh
February	**luty**	**loo**-ti
March	**marzec**	**ma**-zhets
April	**kwiecień**	**kfye**-chen
May	**maj**	may
June	**czerwiec**	**cher**-vyets
July	**lipiec**	**lee**-pyets
August	**sierpień**	**sher**-pyen
September	**wrzesień**	**vzhe**-shen
October	**październik**	pazh-**djer**-neek
November	**listopad**	lees-**to**-pat
December	**grudzień**	**groo**-djen

Seasons

spring	**wiosna**	**vyos**-na
summer	**lato**	**la**-to
autumn	**jesień**	**ye**-shen
winter	**zima**	**zhee**-ma

What is today's date?	**Którego jest dzisiaj?** ktoo-**re**-go yest **djee**-shay?
What day is it today?	**Jaki jest dzisiaj dzień?** **ya**-ki yest **djee**-shay djen?
It's the 5th of March 2007	**Jest piąty marca dwa tysiące siódmego roku** yest pyon-**ti mar**-tsa dva ti-**shon**-tse shood-**me**-go **ro**-koo
on Saturday	**w sobotę** f so-**bo**-te
on Saturdays	**w soboty** f so-**bo**-ti
every Saturday	**w każdą sobotę** f **kazh**-dow so-**bo**-te
this Saturday	**w tą sobotę** f tow so-**bo**-te
next Saturday	**w następną sobotę** v nas-**tem**-pnow so-**bo**-te
last Saturday	**w ostatnią sobotę** v os-**tat** nyow so-**bo**-te
in June	**w czerwcu** f **cher**-ftsoo
at the beginning of June	**na początku czerwca** na po-**chont**-koo **cherf**-tsa
at the end of June	**w końcu czerwca** f **kon**-tsoo **cherf**-tsa

before summer	**przed latem** pshed la-tem
during the summer	**w ciągu lata** f**chon**-goo **la**-ta
after summer	**po lecie** po **le**-che

Time

The 24-hour clock is used a lot more in Poland than in Britain. After 12.00 midday, it continues: **1300 - trzynasta**, **1400 - czternasta**, **1500 - piętnasta**, etc. until **2400 - dwudziesta czwarta**. With the 24-hour clock you say the number of minutes after the hour:

13:30 (1.30 pm)	**trzynasta trzydzieści**
22:45 (10.45 pm)	**dwudziesta druga czterdzieści pięć**

What time is it, please?	**Przepraszam, która godzina?** pshe-**pra**-sham **ktoo**-ra go-**djee**-na?

It's...	**jest...** yest...
2 o'clock	**druga** **droo**-ga
3 o'clock	**trzecia** **tshe**-cha
6 o'clock	**szósta** **shoos**-ta
It's 1 o'clock	**Jest pierwsza** yest **pyerf**-sha
It's midday	**jest południe** yest po-**wood**-nye
It's midnight	**jest północ** yest **poow**-nots
9	**dziewiąta** dje-**vyon**-ta
9.10	**dziesięć po dziewiątej** **dje**-shench po dje-**vyon**-tey
quarter past 9	**piętnaście po dziewiątej** pyet-**nash**-che po dje-**vyon**-tey
9.20	**dwadzieścia po dziewiątej** dva-**djesh**-cha po dje-**vyon**-tey
9.30	**w pół do dziesiątej** f poow do dje-**shon**-tey

9.35	**za dwadzieścia pięć dziesiąta** za dva-**djesh**-shcha pyench dje-**shon**-ta
quarter to 10	**za piętnaście dziesiąta** za pyen-**tnash**-che dje-**shon**-ta
5 to 10	**za pięć dziesiąta** za pyench dje-**shon**-ta

Time phrases

When does it open/close?	**Kiedy jest otwarte/ zamknięte?** **kye**-di yest ot-**far**-te/ zam-**knyen**-te?
When does it begin/finish?	**Kiedy (to) się zaczyna/ kończy?** **kye**-di (to) she za-**chi**-na/ **kon**-chi?
at 3 o'clock	**o trzeciej** o **tshe**-chey
before 3 o'clock	**przed trzecią** pshet **tshe**-chow

after 3 o'clock	**po trzeciej**
	po **tshe**-chey
today	**dzisiaj**
	djee-shay
tonight	**dzisiaj wieczorem**
	djee-shay vye-**cho**-rem
tomorrow	**jutro**
	yoot-ro
yesterday	**wczoraj**
	fcho-ray

Eating out

Eating places

Traditionally, the main meal in Poland is **obiad** which is a dinner/lunch, served between 2.00 pm and 5.00 pm. The evening meal is called **kolacja**. It is lighter than **obiad**, and is served between 7.00 pm and 9.00 pm. However, with changing work habits, more and more people have their main meal in the evenings. In the morning, you have **śniadanie** (breakfast), usually served between 7.00 am and 10.00 am.

Bar-Cafè Many bars serve food such as salads, sandwiches, baguettes and pizzas.

Pizzeria Pizzas. Take-away food, **na wynos**, is also popular.

Piekarnia Bread and cake shops. These sometimes have a café attached where you can try the cakes.

Bar Bistro These are small cafeterias or restaurants that serve hot and cold dishes and salads. Good for quick meals.

Bar mleczny Milk Bar that specialize in dairy products and serve cheap food, suitable for breakfasts or quick lunches.

Cocktail Bar Bars serving milkshakes, ice-cream, cakes and coffee, but not alcoholic cocktails.

Bufet These small restaurants, often attached to railway or bus stations, serve snacks and simple hot food, beer and soft drinks.You can also have a **bufet** on a train, while international and express trains have **wagon restauracyjny** (a restaurant car) serving à la carte meals.

Kawiarnia Coffee places which serve hot and cold drinks and cakes, and sometimes light meals and alcoholic drinks.

Winiarnia/Pub As well as drinks, they sometimes serve light snacks.

Zajazd *or* **Karczma** A country inn. These are often found in the countryside, close to main roads. They offer inexpensive regional meals and sometimes accommodation.

Restauracja The menu and prices are usually displayed outside the entrance. Restaurants are open from about midday to 10.30 pm.

In a bar/café

If you ask for a cup of tea, it will automatically be served without milk, so you need to ask for milk separately. In big cities as many types of coffee are available as abroad.

kawa biała (z mlekiem) **ka**-va **bya**-wa (**z mle**-kyem)	white coffee (with milk)
kawa czarna (bez mleka) **ka**-va **char**-na (bez **mle**-ka)	black coffee (without milk)
ekspresowa ex-pre-**so**-va	espresso (strong small black coffee)
cappuccino ka-poo-**chee**-no	cappuccino

FACE TO FACE

A **Co mogę podać?**
tso **mo**-ge **po**-dach?
What will you have?

B **herbatę z mlekiem, proszę**
her-**ba**-te z **mle**-kyem, **pro**-she
A tea with milk, please

a coffee	**kawa** **ka**-va
a lager	**piwo** **pee**-vo
an orangeade	**oranżada** o-ran-**zha**-da

with lemon	**z cytryną**
	s tsit-**ri**-now
no sugar	**bez cukru**
	bes **tsook**-roo
for two	**dwa razy**
	dva **ra**-zi
for me	**dla mnie**
	dla mnye
for him/her	**dla niego/niej**
	dla **nye**-go/nyey
for us	**dla nas**
	dla nas
with ice	**z lodem**
	z lo-dem
a bottle of mineral water	**butelka wody mineralnej**
	boo-**tel**-ka **vo**-di mee-ne-**ral**-ney
sparkling	**z gazem**
	z ga-zem
still	**bez gazu**
	bez **ga**-zoo

Other drinks to try

sok owocowy fruit juice
czekolada na gorąco hot chocolate
wódka vodka
kwas non-alcoholic slightly fermented drink
kwaśne mleko soured milk
maślanka buttermilk

Reading the menu

If you were planning to eat a full Polish meal, you would begin with the starter, **przekąska**, followed by the first course, **pierwsze danie** (often soup), then the second course, **główne danie** (meat or fish), and end with fruit or **deser** (dessert). This requires some time, so people often skip one or two of the courses. In a restaurant, any of the following three words can be used for menu: **karta, menu, jadłospis**.

In a restaurant

FACE TO FACE

A **Czy mogę zarezerwować stolik na ... osoby?**
chi **mo**-ge za-re-zer-**vo**-vach **sto**-leek na ... o-**so**-bi?
I'd like to book a table for ... people?

B **Tak, na kiedy?**
tak na **kye**-di?
Yes, when for?

A **Na dzisiaj wieczór/na jutro wieczór/ na ósmą wieczór**
na **djee**-shay **vye**-choor/na **yoot**-ro **vye**-choor/ na **oos**-mow **vye**-choor
for this evening/for tomorrow evening/at 8 o'clock in the evening

The menu, please	**Proszę kartę/menu** **pro**-she **kar**-te/me-**nee**
What is the dish of the day?	**Jakie jest danie dnia?** **ya**-kye yest **da**-nye dnya?
Do you have a tourist menu?	**Czy jest zestaw turystyczny?** chi yest **zes**-taf too-ris-**tich**-ni?
at a set price?	**Ze stałą ceną?** ze **sta**-wow **tse**-now?

In a restaurant

What is the speciality of the house?	**Jaka jest specjalność zakładu?** **ya**-ka yest spe-tsyal-noshch zak-**wa**-doo?
Could you tell me what this is?	**Czy może me pan/pani powiedzieć co to jest?** chi **moz**-he mee pan/**pa**-nee po-**vye**-djech tso to yest?
I'll have this	**Poproszę to** po-**pro**-she toh
Could I have some more bread/ water, please?	**Proszę jeszcze trochę chleba/wody** **pro**-she **yesh**-che **tro**-he **hle**-ba/**vo**-di
The bill, please	**Proszę rachunek** **pro**-she ra-**hoo**-nek
Is service included?	**Czy obsługa jest wliczona?** chi op-**swoo**-ga yest vlee-**cho**-na?

Eating out

Vegetarian

Vegetarian dishes are becoming increasingly popular in Poland, and most places offer some meatless dishes.

Are there any vegetarian restaurants here?	**Czy jest tu gdzieś restauracja wegetariańska?** chi yest too gdjesh res-taoo-**ra**-tsya ve-ge-tar-**yan**-ska?
Do you have any vegetarian dishes?	**Czy są dania wegetariańskie?** chi sow **da**-nya ve-ge-tar-**yan**-skye?
Which dishes have no meat/fish?	**Które dania są bez mięsa/ryby?** ktoo-re **da**-nya sow bez **myen**-sa/**ri**-bi?
What fish dishes do you have?	**Jakie są dania rybne?** **ya**-kye sow **da**-nya **rib**-ne?
I'd like dumplings as a main course	**Proszę pierogi jako główne danie** **pro**-she pye-**ro**-gee **ya**-ko **gwoov**-ne **da**-nye

Vegetarian

I don't eat meat	**Nie jem mięsa** nye yem **myen**-sa
What do you recommend?	**Co pan/pani poleca?** tso pan/**pa**-nee po-**le**-tsa?
Is it made with vegetable stock?	**Czy to jest na bazie jarzyn?** chi to yest na **ba**-zhe **ya**-zhin?

Possible dishes

Pierogi stuffed dumplings

z kapustą i grzybami with cabbage and mushrooms

z serem with cheese

leniwe with flour, mashed potatoes and white cheese

Placki kartoflane potato pancakes made with grated raw potatoes and onions, fried and served with cream

Sałatka jarzynowa a salad of cooked vegetables, served with cream and mayonnaise dressing

Sałatka kartoflana potato salad

Wines and spirits

The wine list, please	**Proszę listę win** **pro**-she **lees**-te veen
white wine	**białe** **bya**-we
red wine	**czerwone** cher-**vo**-ne
Can you recommend a good wine?	**Czy poleca pan/pani jakieś dobre wino?** chi po-**le**-ca pan/p**a**-nee **ya**-kyesh **dob**-re **vee**-no?
A bottle...	**Proszę butelkę** **pro**-she boo-**tel**-ke
a carafe...	**karafkę** ka-**raf**-ke
of house wine	**wina stołowego** **vee**-na sto-wo-**ve**-go

Wines

Poland is not a wine producing country. Traditionally, vodka and beer are the main drinks, but increasingly more and more people drink wine. The cheapest wines come from Hungary, Romania and Bulgaria, but other wines are available in bigger supermarkets. Good restaurants may offer many varieties of good wines.

Wino białe/czerwone white/red wine
Wino słodkie sweet wine
Wino wytrawne dry wine
Wino pół-słodkie semi-sweet wine
Wino pół-wytrawne semi-dry wine
Wino musujące sparkling wine
Wino stołowe table wine
Szampan Champagne

Spirits and liqueurs

Vodka, **wódka**, made from potatoes or rye, is a national drink. People drink it on many occasions. It can be **czysta** (non-flavoured) or flavoured. It is drunk from small glasses, always with a little snack.

Types of vodka and other spirits:

jarzębiak rowanberry vodka
myśliwska hunter's vodka
cytrynówka lemon-flavoured vodka
żubrówka bison vodka
śliwowica plum brandy
winiak Polish cognac
miód pitny mead

Menu reader

bakłażan aubergine
baranina mutton
barszcz beetroot soup
befsztyk beef steak
bezy meringue
bigos traditional hunter's dish, made with sauerkraut and various meats
bita śmietana whipped cream
botwinka beetroot soup made with young beetroot leaves
brukselka Brussel sprouts
budyń custard-type dessert
bułka bread roll
buraczki beetroot
cebula onion
chleb bread
chłodnik litewski cold beetroot soup with yoghurt and dill
chrzan horseradish
ciastko a slice of cake
ciasto cake

cielęcina veal
cukier sugar
cukinia courgette/marrow
cytryna lemon
cytrynówka lemon-flavoured vodka
czarna (kawa) black (coffee)
czekolada chocolate
czekolada pitna drinking chocolate
czerwone (wino) red (wine)
czosnek garlic
duszone stewed (meat)
dziczyzna game meat
fasola po bretońsku baked beans
fasola szparagowa French beans
flaki tripe
frytki French fries
galaretka owocowa fruit jelly
gęś pieczona roast goose
golonka cured and boiled ham on the bone
gołąbki minced meat and rice wrapped in cabbage leaves
grochówka pea soup served with pieces of sausage
groszek peas
grzanka toast
grzyby (wild) mushrooms

gorący hot
gruszka w sosie czekoladowym pear in chocolate sauce
gulasz goulash
herbata tea
herbatniki biscuits
indyk turkey
jadłospis menu
jagody blueberries
jajko egg
jajko gotowane na miękko/twardo egg (soft boiled/hard boiled)
jajecznica scrambled eggs
jarzębiak rowanberry vodka
jarzynowa zupa vegetable soup
kaczka pieczona z jabłkami roast duck with baked apples
kalafior cauliflower
kanapka sandwich
kapusta kiszona sauerkraut
kapuśniak sauerkraut soup
karp w galarecie carp in aspic
karta menu
kartoflanka potato soup
kasza gryczana roasted buckwheat

kiełbasa sausage
kisiel jelly-type dessert
klopsiki meatballs
kluski pasta or noodles
kompot compote (stewed fruit drink)
kolacja supper
koperek dill
kopytka potato dumplings
kotlet meat cutlet/chop
kotlet schabowy breaded pork cutlet
kurczak chicken
kuropatwa partridge
lody ice-cream
łosoś salmon
łosoś wędzony smoked salmon
makowiec poppy seed cake
masło butter
maślanka buttermilk
mizeria cucumber salad in sour cream
nadzienie stuffing
naleśniki z serem i ze śmietaną pancakes with white cheese and cream
maliny raspberries
marchew carrots
mięso meat (in general)

mięso z rusztu grilled meat
napoje alkoholowe/bezalkoholowe alcoholic/non-alcoholic drinks
napoje gorące/chłodzące hot/cold drinks
nóżki w galarecie pig's trotters in aspic
obiad dinner (usually eaten at lunchtime)
ogórki kiszone cucumbers in brine
orzechy nuts
ostry sharp/spicy
owoce fruit
owoce morza seafood
owsianka porridge
ozór tongue
panierowany breaded
parówki frankfurters
paszteciki small pastries filled with meat or mushrooms
pasztet paté
pączek doughnut
pieczarki smażone fried button mushrooms
pieczeń roast meat
pieczywo breads, rolls, croissants, etc.
pieprz pepper (condiment)
piernik ginger cake
pierogi dumplings stuffed with a variety of fillings, they can be served savoury or sweet:

z kapustą i grzybami with sauerkraut and mushrooms
leniwe with potatoes and cheese
z mięsem with meat
z owocami with fruit filling
z serem with cheese
pierś kurczaka chicken breast
piwo jasne/ciemne light/dark beer
placki ziemniaczane potato pancakes
placek tart/pie (sweet)
plaster/plasterek slice
płatki śniadaniowe breakfast cereals
polędwica sirloin (a cold cut of meat), can be smoked or boiled
pomidor tomato
porcja portion
potrawa meal
prosiak piglet
przekąski starters
przyprawy seasoning
pulpety meatballs
pyzy regional round potato dumplings
rabarbar rhubarb
rak (freshwater) crayfish
razowy chleb black rye bread
rodzynki raisins

rolmopsy pickled herrings
rosół clear chicken broth
rosół z makaronem clear chicken broth with noodles
ryba fish
ryż rice
rzodkiewka radish
sałata green lettuce
sałatka salad
sałatka jarzynowa vegetable salad (usually cooked vegetables, in a mayonnaise dressing)
sałatka z kapusty cabbage salad
sandacz pike-perch
sarnina deer meat
schab pieczony roast pork loin
seler celery root
seler naciowy celery sticks
ser cheese
  biały fresh soft white cheese
  żółty hard yellow cheese
  miękki soft cheese
  owczy ewe's cheese
  kozi goat's cheese
  topiony processed cheese
sernik cheesecake
słodki sweet

smażony fried
soczewica lentils
sok juice
  pomarańczowy orange juice
  owocowy fruit juice
  jarzynowy vegetable juice
  z marchwi carrot juice
  pomidorowy tomato juice
  z czarnej porzeczki blackcurrant juice
sos sauce
  koperkowy dill sauce
  grzybowy mushroom sauce
specjalność dnia speciality of the day
specjalność zakładu speciality of the house
surówka salad of raw vegetables
szarlotka apple pie
szaszłyk kebab
szczaw sorrel
szynka ham
szczupak pike
szczypiorek chives
sznycel breaded pork or veal cutlet
szynka ham
  wędzona smoked ham
  gotowana boiled ham

śledź herring
  śledź w śmietanie herring in sour cream
  śledź w oleju herring in oil
ślimaki snails
śliwki plums
śliwowica plum brandy
śmietana cream
śniadanie breakfast
świeży fresh
tłusty fat, fatty
tort gateau
truskawki strawberries
tuńczyk tuna fish
twarożek/twaróg fresh soft white cheese
wędzony smoked
węgorz eel
wątróbka liver
wędliny cooked cold meats
wieprzowina pork
winiak Polish brandy
wino wine
wołowina beef
wiśnie sour cherries
woda water
wódka vodka

zając w śmietanie hare in sour cream
zakąski appetizers/snacks, often with vodka
zestaw set meal
  zestaw śniadaniowy set breakfast
  zestaw obiadowy set dinner
zielona sałata green lettuce
ziemniaki potatoes
  gotowane boiled potatoes
  puree mashed potatoes
  pieczone baked potatoes
  w mundurkach jacket potatoes/in skins
zrazy zawijane stuffed, rolled beef
z rusztu grilled
zupa soup
  grzybowa mushroom soup
  jarzynowa vegetable soup
  pomidorowa tomato soup
  szczawiowa sorrel soup
  owocowa fruit soup
żeberka spare ribs
żur/żurek z kiełbasą sour rye soup with white sausage
żółty ser hard yellow cheese
żubrówka bison vodka
zestaw set menu

Grammar

Nouns

Words such as car, horse, book or Maria are **nouns** and are used to refer to a person or thing. All Polish nouns have a grammatical gender: masculine, feminine or neuter. For example, **kobieta** (woman) is feminine **chłopiec** (boy) is masculine and **dziecko** (child) is neuter. However, in most cases the grammatical gender is not related to its meaning and is determined only by the ending of the noun.

Most masculine nouns end in a consonant: **pies** (dog), **obraz** (painting), **rok** (year). Some exceptions are masculine nouns ending in -**a**, such as **mężczyzna** (man), **kierowca** (driver). Most nouns ending in -**a** are feminine: **książka** (book), **praca** (work), but some nouns ending in a consonant are feminine: **solidarność** (solidarity), **noc** (night). All feminine first names end in -**a**:

Alicja, **Katarzyna**. The same rule applies to feminine surnames ending in **-ska**, **-cka**: for example, **Danuta Kownacka**.
Neuter nouns end in **-o**, **-e**, *or* **-ę**: **okno**, (window), **morze** (sea), **imię** (first name).

Polish is characterized by its case system, which means that each noun and words that describe them may appear in any of the seven cases listed below, depending on what is being expressed in a sentence. The complexity of the case system means that each noun can have as many as twelve different endings, although some endings are repeated. The best way is to try to recognize the main part of the word and learn the words as they appear in the phrases.

Nominative (the dictionary form)

The subject of the sentence – a person or thing performing the action, or in introductions following **to jest**... (this is...), e.g. **to jest mój <u>syn</u>** (this is my son).

Accusative

The direct object of the sentence: **odwiedzam mojego syna** (I'm visiting my son).

Genitive

To express possession: **żona mojego syna** (my son's wife); after negation: **nie ma mojego syna** ; after expressions of quantity: **mam dwóch synów** (I have two sons); after some prepositions: **jadę do mojego syna** (I'm going to my son's).

Dative

The indirect object, a person or thing to whom something happens: **dałam prezent mojemu synowi** (I gave a present to my son).

Instrumental

Points to the instrument with which something is done; doing something together: **mieszkam razem z moim synem** (I live together with my son).

Locative

Used only after certain prepositions: **rozmawiamy o moim synu** (we're talking about my son).

Vocative

Used in the direct form of address, often with first names, eg. **Basiu**, **mamo**.

Plurals

Plurals of nouns are formed in a variety of ways, depending on the gender and on the last letter of the noun, resulting in a number of different endings. Again, it is best not to worry too much about the plural endings at this stage and try to remember words as they appear in the phrases.

Polish does not have articles (**a** and **the**) in front of the nouns.

Adjectives

An adjective is a word such as small, pretty or practical that describes a person or thing, or gives extra information about them. They agree in number and gender with the noun they are describing. In the nominative case singular they have the following endings: **-i**, **-y** in masculine; **-a** in feminine; and **-e** in neuter:

drogi samochod (expensive car)
duży dom (big house)
ładna pogoda (nice weather)
spokojne morze (calm sea)

Adjective endings change according to which case is being used (what you want to say), e.g. **nie ma ładnej pogody** (the weather isn't good); **jeżdżę tanim samochodem** (I'm driving a cheap car).

In the dictionary only the masculine singular form is included.

In plural nominative the adjectives end in **-e** *or* **-i**: **białe domy** (white houses); **przystojni mężczyźni** (handsome men). Surnames ending in **-ski**, **-cki** (masculine) and **-ska**, **-cka** (feminine) also behave like adjectives: **to jest pan Białecki** (this is Mr Białecki); **pana Białeckiego nie ma w biurze** (Mr Białecki is not in the office).

Pronouns

Personal pronouns

A personal pronoun is a word that you use to refer to someone or something when you do not need to use a noun, often because the person or thing has been mentioned earlier. They are words such as **I**, **you**, **he**, **she**, **it**, **we**, **they**.

Singular (Nominative)		Plural (Nominative)	
I	**ja**	we	**my**
you	**ty**	you	**wy**
he	**on**	they	**oni** (masculine human)
she	**ona**	they	**one** (women, children and things)
it	**ono**		

Personal pronouns have different forms in different cases, e.g. **on chce się ze mną bawić** (he wants to play with me); **kup jej prezent** (buy her a present).

Personal pronouns are often omitted in Polish, since the verb ending itself always distinguishes the person:

mieszkam	I live
mieszkasz	you live
mieszkają	they live

Possessive pronouns

my, your, his, her, our, their

These words depend on the gender and number of the noun they accompany, and not on the sex of the 'owner'.

	Singular (Nominative) masculine	feminine	neuter	Plural (Nominative) masculine human	others
my	mój	moja	moje	moi	moje
your	twój	twoja	teoje	twoi	twoje
his	jego	jego	jego	jego	jego
her	jej	jej	jej	jej	jej
its	jego	jego	jego	jego	jego
our	nasz	nasza	nazse	nasi	nazse
your	wasz	wasza	wasze	wasi	wasze
their	ich	ich	ich	ich	ich

Again, they have different forms depending on the case used, e.g. **Nie widzę naszych dzieci** (I can't see our children).

Demonstrative pronouns

this, that, these, those

They appear in front of the noun they are pointing to and agree grammatically with its gender and number.

Singular masculine	feminine	neuter	Plural masc. human	others
ten	ta	to	ci	te

Examples:

ten chłopiec	(this boy)
ci chłopcy	(these boys)
ta dziewczyna	(this girl)
te dziewczyny	(these girls)
to dziecko	(this child)
te dzieci	(these children)

As with previous words, they have different forms in different cases: **lubię tych studentów** (I like these students).

Verbs

A verb is a word such as sing, walk or cry which is used with a subject to say what someone or something does, or what happens to them. Verbs have different endings according to person, number (singular and plural), tense (present, past and future) and gender (in the past tense only). That is why in this book two past forms (masculine and feminine) are given where necessary, e.g. **czytał** (he was reading) **and czytała** (she was reading). The last consonant of the infinitive form (dictionary form) of all verbs ends in -ć, e.g. **pisać** (to write); **czytać** (to read).

A typical feature of Polish verbs is that most of them have two different forms in the infinitive: in the past and in the future tense. This corresponds with the fact of completion of the action (perfective form) or incompletion (imperfective form). For this reason the verb form encountered in spoken or written Polish can be quite different from its dictionary form, e.g. **czytać** (to read in general) and **przeczytać** (to finish reading something). Sometimes the verbs can look totally unrelated, e.g.

Grammar

brać (to take something on a regular basis) and wziąć (a one-off action of taking something).

In addition, there are two forms of the verb of motion 'to go': iść (to go on foot), and jechać (to go by transport).

There are four main patterns for verb endings, based on the 1st and 2nd person singular endings in the present tense. Both regular and irregular verbs are included here, since they can share the same endings (irregular verbs refer to changes in the middle form of the verb, not the endings).

1st person singular	2nd person singular	
-ę	-esz	piszę, piszesz (I'm writing, you're writing)
-ę	-isz/ysz	robię, robisz, krzyczę, krzyczysz (to do, to scream)
-am	-asz	kocham, kochasz (to love)
-em	-esz	jem, jesz (to eat)

The following are some examples. Personal pronouns are only used if you need to emphasize the person who is speaking, otherwise the verb ending specifies the person.

	pisać	**to write**
(ja)	piszę	I write
(ty)	piszesz	you write
(on/ona/ono)	pisze	(s)he/it writes
(my)	piszemy	we write
(wy)	piszecie	you write
(oni/one)	piszą	they write

past participle pisany (with być)

	mówić	**to speak**
(ja)	mówię	I speak
(ty)	mówisz	you speak
(on/ona/ono)	mówi	(s)he/it speaks
(my)	mówimy	we speak
(wy)	mówicie	you speak
(oni/one)	mówią	they speak

past participle mówiony (with być)

	czytać	**to read**
(ja)	czytam	I read
(ty)	czytasz	you read
(on/ona/ono)	czyta	(s)he/it reads
(my)	czytamy	we read
(wy)	czytacie	you read
(oni/one)	czytają	they read

Past participle **czytany** (with **być**)

	rozumieć	**to understand**
(ja)	rozumiem	I understand
(ty)	rozumiesz	you understand
(on/ona/ono)	rozumie	(s)he/it understands
(my)	rozumiemy	we understand
(wy)	rozumiecie	you understand
(oni/one)	rozumieją	they understand

Past participle **rozumiany** (with **być**)

Irregular Verbs are those in which the middle part is different to its dictionary form.

Among the most important irregular verbs are the following:

	być	**to be**
(ja)	**jestem**	I am
(ty)	**jesteś**	you are
(on/ona/ono)	**jest**	(s)he/it is
(my)	**jesteśmy**	we are
(wy)	**jesteście**	you are
(oni/one)	**są**	they are

	mieć	**to have**
(ja)	**mam**	I have
(ty)	**masz**	you have
(on/ona/ono)	**ma**	(s)he/it has
(my)	**mamy**	we have
(wy)	**macie**	you have
(oni/one)	**mają**	they have

	iść	**to go (on foot)**
(ja)	**idę**	I go
(ty)	**idziesz**	you go
(on/ona/ono)	**idzie**	(s)he/it goes
(my)	**idziemy**	we go
(wy)	**idziecie**	you go
(oni/one)	**idą**	they go

	jechać	**to go (by transport)**
(ja)	jadę	I go
(ty)	jedziesz	you go
(on/ona/ono)	jedzie	(s)he/it goes
(my)	jedziemy	we go
(wy)	jedziecie	you go
(oni/one)	jadą	they go

	chcieć	**to want**
(ja)	chcę	I want
(ty)	chcesz	you want
(on/ona/ono)	chce	(s)he/it wants
(my)	chcemy	we want
(wy)	chcecie	you want
(oni/one)	chcą	they want

	brać	**to take**
(ja)	biorę	I take
(ty)	bierzesz	you take
(on/ona/ono)	bierze	(s)he/it takes
(my)	bierzemy	we take
(wy)	bierzecie	you take
(oni/one)	biorą	they take

Past tense

All verbs take the same endings in the past tense and they follow gender distinctions, apart from the plural. Plural endings for the masculine human differ from all others. To form the past tense, just drop the final -ć from the infinitive and add the following endings:

Singular **masculine**	**feminine**	**neuter**	**Plural** **masc. human**	**all others**
-łem	-łam	—	-liśmy	-łyśmy
-łeś	-łaś	—	-liście	-łyście
-ł	-ła	-ło	-li	-ły

Example:

	pisać	**to write**
(ja)	pisałem	I wrote (man)
	ja pisałam	I wrote (woman)

(ja)	pisałem/łam	I wrote
(ty)	pisałeś/łaś	you wrote
(on/ona/ono)	pisał/pisała/ pisało	(s)he, it wrote
(my)	pisaliśmy/ łyśmy	we wrote

(wy)	**pisaliście/ łyście**	you wrote
(oni)	**pisali**	they wrote (men)
(one)	**pisały**	they wrote (women)

Therefore the commonly used expression 'I'd like to' has two versions in Polish, since it has a past tense component: **chciałbym** (man speaking) and **chciałabym** (woman speaking).

Public holidays

On national holidays places such as museums may have shorter opening hours, and information offices may be closed. Public transport may run a limited service. Apart from Easter Monday and Corpus Christi, which change each year, all the holidays keep to the same date.

1 January	**Nowy Rok** New Year's Day
March/April	**Wielkanoc** Easter
1 May	**Pierwszy Maja** May Day
3 May	**Konstytucja 3 Maja** Constitution Day
Thursday in May/June	**Boże Ciało** Corpus Christi
15 August	**Wniebowzięcie** Assumption
1 November	**Wszystkich Świętych** All Saints Day
11 November	**Dzień Niepodległości** Independence Day
25 and 26 December	**Boże Narodzenie** Christmas

English – Polish

A

English	Polish	Pronunciation
about	o; około	o; o-**ko**-wo
above	nad`	nat
abroad	za granicą	za gra-**nee**-tsow
accelerator	pedał gazu	**pe**-daw **ga**-zoo
to accept	przyjmować	pshiy-**mo**-vach
do you accept credit cards?	czy przyjmujecie karty kredytowe?	chi pshiy-moo-**ye**-che **kar**-ti kre-di-**to**-ve?
accident	wypadek	vi-**pa**-dek
accidentally	przypadkowo	pshi-pat-**ko**-vo
accommodation	zakwaterowanie	zak-fa-te-ro-**van**-ye
ache	ból	bool
across	przez	pshes
adaptor (electricity)	adapter	a-**dap**-ter
address	adres	**ad**-res
what's your address?	adres; proszę?	**ad**-res; **pro**-she?
admission	wstęp	fstemp
admission charge	opłata za wstęp	op-**wa**-ta za fstemp
admission fee	wstęp wolny	fstemp **vo**-lni
adult	dorosły	do-**ros**-wi
aeroplane	samolot	sa-**mo**-lot
a few of...	kilka...	**keel**-ka...
afraid: *to be afraid*	bać się	bach she
after	po	po

afternoon po południu po po-**wood**-nyoo
good afternoon dzień dobry djen **dob**-ri
in the afternoon po południu po po-**wood**-nyou
this afternoon dzisiaj po południu **djee**-shay po po-**wood**-nyou
tomorrow afternoon jutro po południu **yoo**-tro po po-**wood**-nyou
afterwards potem **po**-tem
again znowu **zno**-voo
age wiek vyek
ago temu **te**-moo
to agree zgadzać się **zga**-dzach she
air powietrze po-**vyet**-she

air conditioning klimatyzacja klee-ma-ti-**za**-tsya
is there air conditioning? czy jest klimatyzacja? chi yest klee-ma-ti-**za**-tsya?
airmail (post) lotnicza lo-**tnee**-cha
airport lotnisko lot-**nees**-ko
alarm clock budzik **boo**-djeek
alcohol alkohol al-**ko**-hol
all; everything wszystko **fshis**-tko
all right w porządku f po-**zhon**-tkoo
allergy uczulenie oo-choo-**le**-nye
allowed dozwolone doz-vo-**lo**-ne
already już yoosh
also też tesh
a.m. przed południem pshet po-**wood**-nyem

English	Polish	Pronunciation
ambulance	pogotowie ratunkowe	po-go-**to**-vye ra-toon-**ko**-ve
America	Ameryka	a-**me**-ri-ka
American (person, man)	Amerykanin	a-me-ri-**ka**-neen
American (woman)	Amerykanka	a-me-ri-**kan**-ka
amount	ilość	**ee**-loschch
and	i	ee
angry	zły	zwi
animal	zwierzę	**zvye**-zhe
ankle	kostka	**kos**-tka
anniversary	rocznica	roch-**nee**-tsa
to annoy	irytować	ee-ri-**to**-vach
another one	inny	**een**-ni
answer	odpowiedź	ot-**po**-vyech
to answer	odpowiedzieć	ot-po-**vye**-djech
answerphone	automatyczna sekretarka	au-to-ma-teech-na se-kre-**tar**-ka
antibiotics	antybiotyki	an-ti-byo-**ti**-kee
I'm on antibiotics	jestem na antybiotykach	**yes**-tem na an-ti-byo-**ti**-kah
anybody	ktoś; każdy	ktosh; **kazh**-di
anything else?	czy coś jeszcze?	chi tsosh **yesh**-che?
apart from	oprócz	**op**-rooch
apartment	mieszkanie	myesh-**ka**-nye
to apologize	przepraszać	pshe-**pra**-shach
apples	jabłka	**yap**-ka
appointment	wizyta	vee-**zi**-ta
appointment (to make)	umówić się	oo-**moo**-veech she

apricots	morele	mo-**re**-le
April	kwiecień	**kfye**-chen
area	okolica	o-ko-**lee**-tsa
area code	numer kierunkowy	**noo**-mer kye-roon-**ko**-vi
are there...?	czy są...?	chi sow...?
arm	ramię	**ra**-mye
to arrange	załatwić	za-**wat**-feech
arrival (train)	przyjazd	**phsi**-yast
arrival (flight)	przylot	**pshi**-lot
to arrive (train/plain)	przyjeżdżać/przylecieć	pshi-**yezh**-djach/pshi-**le**-chech
art	sztuka	**shtoo**-ka
art gallery	galeria sztuki	ga-**ler**-ya **shtoo**-kee
to ask	prosić	**pro**-sheech
as soon as possible	możliwie jak najszybciej	mozh-**lee**-vye yak nay-**ship**-chey
ashtray	popielniczka	po-pyel-**neech**-ka
at least	przynajmniej	pshi-**nay**-mnyey
attention	uwaga	oo-**va**-ga
August	sierpień	**sher**-pyen
aunt	ciotka	**chot**-ka
Auschwitz	Oświęcim	osh-**fyen**-cheem
Australia	Australia	a-oos-**tra**-lia
Australian (man)	Australijczyk	a-oos-tra-**leey**-chik
Australian (woman)	Australijka	a-oos-tra-**leey**-ka

Australian	australijski	a-oos-tra-**leeys**-kee
autumn	jesień	**ye**-shen
available	wolny	**vol**-ni
avalanche	lawina	la-**vee**-na
awful	okropny	o-**krop**-ni

B

baby	dziecko	**djet**s-ko
baby food	jedzenie dla dzieci	ye-**dze**-nye dla **dje**-chee
back (part of body)	plecy	**ple**-tsi
backache	ból krzyża	bool **kshi**-zha
backpacking	z plecakiem	s ple-**tsa**-kyem
bacon	boczek	**bo**-chek
bad	zły	zwi
badly	źle	zhle
bag	torba	**tor**-ba
baggage	bagaż	**ba**-gash
baggage check	kontrola bagażu	kon-**tro**-la ba-**ga**-zhoo
baggage claim	odbiór bagażu	**od**-byoor ba-**ga**-zhoo
bakery	piekarnia	pye-**kar**-nya
bakery products	pieczywo	pye-**chi**-vo
bald	łysy	**wi**-si
ball	piłka	**peew**-ka
ballpoint pen	długopis	dwoo-**go**-pees
bandage	bandaż	**ban**-dash
bank	bank	bank

bank account	konto bankowe	**kon**-to ban-**ko**-ve
barber's	fryzjer męski	**fri**-**zyer** **men**-skee
bargains	okazje	o-**ka**-**zye**
basement	piwnica	peev-**nee**-tsa
basketball	koszykówka	ko-shik-**oof**-ka
bath (to take a)	kąpiel	**kom**-**pyel**
bath (tub)	wanna	**van**-na
bathroom	łazienka	wa-**zhen**-ka
to be	być	bich
to be able to...	umieć...	**oo**-myech...
to be allergic	być uczulonym	bich oo-choo-**lo**-nim
to be called (my name is...)	nazywać się	na-**zi**-vach she
to be in working order	działać	**dja**-wach
to be pregnant	być w ciąży	bich **f chon**-zhi
beach	plaża	**pla**-zha
beautiful	piękny	**pyen**-kni
because	bo/ponieważ	bo/po-**nye**-vash
beer	piwo	**pee**-vo
bed	łóżko	**woosh**-ko
bedding	pościel	**posh**-chel
before	przed	phset
to begin	zaczynać	za-**chi**-nach
beginner	początkujący	po-chon-tkoo-**yon**-tsi
behind	za	za
Belarus	Białoruś	bya-**woo**-roosh
to belong	należeć	na-**le**-zhech

English – Polish

best	najlepszy	nay-**lep**-shi
better	lepiej	**le**-pyey
Bialorussian	białoruski	bya-wo-**roos**-kee
bicycle	rower	**ro**-ver
big	duży	**doo**-zhi
bigger	większy	**vyen**-kshi
bill	rachunek	ra-**hoo**-nek
binoculars	lornetka	lor-**net**-ka
birthday	urodziny	oo-ro-**djee**-ni
Happy Birthday	Wszystkiego najlepszego!	fshist-**kye**-go nay-lep-**she**-go!
biscuits	herbatniki	her-bat-**nee**-kee
black	czarny	**cha**-rni
bladder	pęcherz	**pen**-hesh
blanket	koc	kots
bleach	chlorek	**hlo**-rek
blind (sightless)	niewidomy	nye-vee-**do**-mi
blood	krew	kref
blouse, top	bluzka	**bloos**-ka
blue	niebieski	nye-**byes**-kee
boarding card	karta pokładowa	**kar**-ta po-kwa-**do**-va
boat trip	rejs	reys
boiled	gotowany	go-to-**va**-ni
bone	kość	koshch
book	książka	**kshon**-shka
guidebook	przewodnik	pshe-**vod**-neek
to book	zarezerwować	za-re-zer-**vo**-vach
boots	buty	**boo**-ti
boring	nudny	**nood**-ni

to be born urodzić się oo-**ro**-djeech she
to borrow pożyczyć po-**zchi**-chich
bottle butelka boo-**tel**-ka
bowl miska **mees**-ka
box pudełko poo-**dew**-ko
boy chłopiec **hwo**-pyets
boyfriend chłopak **hwo**-pak
brakes hamulce ha-**mool**-tse
bread chleb hlep
bread roll bułka **boow**-ka
break przerwa **psher**-va
to break złamać **zwa**-mach
to break into włamać się **vwa**-mach she
breakfast śniadanie shnya-**da**-nye
what time is breakfast? o której jest śniadanie? o **ktoo**-rey yest shnya-**da**-nye?
breast pierś pyersh
to breathe oddychać od-**di**-hach
bridge most most
Britain Brytania bri-**ta**-nya
British brytyjski bri-**tiy**-skee
British (male) Brytyjczyk bri-**tiy**-chik
British (woman) Brytyjka bri-**ti**y-ka
broken zepsuty zep-**soo**-ti
it's broken to jest zepsute to yest zep-**soo**-te
brown brązowy bron-**zo**-vi
bucket wiadro **vyad**-ro
building budynek boo-**di**-nek
bureau de change kantor **kan**-tor

bus station	dworzec autobusowy	**dvo**-zheths au-to-boo-**so**-vi
bus stop	przystanek autobusowy	phis-**ta**-nek au-to-boo-**so**-vi
busy	zajęty	za-**yen**-ti
but	ale	**a**-le
butcher's	rzeźnik	**zhezh**-neek
butter	masło	**ma**-swo
to buy	kupić	**koo**-peech
bye!	do widzenia!	do vee-**dze**-nya!

C

café	kawiarnia	ka-**vyar**-nya
cake (large)	placek	**pla**-tsek
to call	zawołać	za-**vo**-wach
to be called	nazywać się	na-**zi**-vach she
camera	aparat fotograficzny	a-**pa**-rat fo-to-gra-**feech**-ni
camera shop	sklep fotograficzny	sklep fo-to-gra-**feech**-ni
to camp	obozować	o-bo-**zo**-vach
camping site	kemping	**kem**-peenk
can	puszka	**poosh**-ka
can I/can we...?	czy mogę/czy możemy...?	chi **mo**-ge/chi mo-**zhe**-mi...?
can you...?	czy może pan/pani...?	chi **mo**-zhe pan/**pa**-nee...?
can opener	otwieracz do puszek	ot-**fye**-rach do **poo**-shek
Canada	Kanada	ka-**na**-da
Canadian	kanadyjski	ka-na-**diy**-skee
Canadian (man)	Kanadyjczyk	ka-na-**diy**-chik

Canadian (woman)	Kanadyjka	ka-na-**diy**-ka
canal	kanał	**ka**-naw
to cancel	odwołać	od-**vo**-wach
cancer (illness)	rak	rak
candle	świeczka	**sfyech**-ka
canoe	kajak	**ka**-yak
car	samochód	sa-**mo**-hoot
by car	samochodem	sa-mo-**ho**-dem
car ferry	prom samochodowy	prom sa-mo-ho-**do**-vi
car park	parking	**par**-keenk
car rental	wynajem samochodów	vi-**na**-yem sa-mo-**ho**-doof
car sickness	choroba lokomocyjna	ho-**ro**-ba lo-ko-mo-**tseey**-na
car wash	myjnia samochodowa	**miy**-nya sa-mo-ho-**do**-va
caravan	przyczepa	pshi-**che**-pa
careful	ostrożny	os-**trozh**-ni
carpet	dywan	**di**-van
carrier bag	reklamówka	re-kla-**moof**-ka
cash	gotówka	go-**toof**-ka
cash desk	kasa	**ka**-sa
cash machine	bankomat	ban-**ko**-mat
castle	zamek	**za**-mek
to catch (train)	zdążyć na...	**zdon**-zhich na...
CD	płyta kompaktowa	**pwi**-ta kom-pak-**to**-va
cemetery	cmentarz	**tsmen**-tash
centre of town	śródmieście	shrood-**myesh**-che

English	Polish	Pronunciation
cereal (breakfast)	płatki śniadaniowe	**pwat**-kee shnya-da-**nyo**-ve
chair	krzesło	**kshes**-wo
chair lift	wyciąg krzesełkowy	**vi**-chonk kshe-sew-**ko**-vi
change (money)	drobne	**drob**-ne
changeable	zmienny	**zmyen**-ni
to change money	wymienić pieniądze	vi-**mye**-neech pye-**nyon**-dze
where can I change money?	gdzie mogę wymienić pieniądze?	gdje **mo**-ge vi-**mye**-neech pye-**nyon**-dze?
charge (money)	opłata	op-**wa**-ta
cheap	tani	**ta**-nee
to check	sprawdzić	**sprav**-djeech
to check in	przejść przez kontrolę	psheyshch pshes kon-**tro**-le
check-in	odprawa	ot-**pra**-va
check-in desk	stanowisko	sta-no-**vees**-ko
cheek (part of body)	policzek	po-**lee**-chek
cheers!	na zdrowie!	na **zdro**-vye!
cheese	ser	ser
chemist's	apteka	ap-**te**-ka
cheque	czek	chek
cheque book	książeczka czekowa	kshon-**zhech**-ka che-**ko**-va
chicken	kurczak	**koor**-chak
child/children	dziecko/dzieci	**djets**-ko/**dje**-chee
chips	frytki	**frit**-kee

chocolate	czekolada	che-ko-**la**-da
church	kościół	**kosh**-choow
Christmas	Boże Narodzenie	**bo**-zhe na-ro-**dze**-nye
cigarettes	papierosy	pa-pye-**ro**-si
cinema	kino	**kee**-no
city, town	miasto	**myas**-to
clean	czysty	**chi**-sti
clever	mądry	**mon**-dri
climbing	wspinaczka	fspee-**nach**-ka
cling-film	folia	**fo**-lya
cloakroom	szatnia	**shat**-nya
clock	zegar	**ze**-gar
to close	zamykać	za-**mi**-kach
closed	zamknięte	zam-**knyen**-te
clothes	odzież; ubranie	**o**-djesh; oo-**bra**-nye
clouds	chmury	**hmoo**-ri
coach	autokar	au-**to**-kar
coach trip	wycieczka autokarowa	vi-**chech**-ka au-to-ka-**ro**-va
coat	płaszcz	pwashch
coffee	kawa	**ka**-va
cold	zimny	**zhim**-ni
cold (illness)	przeziębienie	pshe-zhem-**bye**-nye
cold meats	wędliny	ven-**dlee**-ni
collection (of luggage)	odbiór bagażu	**od**-byoor ba-**ga**-zhoo
comb	grzebień	**gzhe**-byen

English	Polish	Pronunciation
to come (on foot/by transport)	przyjść/ przyjechać	pshyschch/ pshi-**ye**-hach
compartment (train)	przedział	**pshe**-djaw
complaint (about a purchase)	reklamacja	re-kla-**mats**-ya
complaint (about a service)	zażalenie	za-zha-**le**-nye
concentration camp	obóz koncentra-cyjny	**o**-boos kon-tsen-tra-**tsiy**-ni
concession/ with concession	ulga/ulgowy	**ool**-ga/ool-**go**-vi
conditioner	odżywka	od-**zhif**-ka
conductor (on train)	konduktor	kon-**doo**-ktor
confirm	potwierdzić	po-**tfyer**-djeech
connection	połączenie	po-won-**che**-nye
constipation	zatwardzenie	zat-far-**dze**-nye
to contact	skontaktować się	skon-tak-**to**-vach she
contact lenses	szkła/soczewki kontaktowe	shkwa/so-**chef**-kee kon-tak-**to**-ve
contraceptives	środki antykoncep-cyjne	**shrot**-kee an-ti-kon-tsep-**tsiy**-ne
corkscrew	korkociąg	kor-**ko**-chonk
to cook	gotować	go-**to**-vach
cooker	kuchenka	koo-**hen**-ka

to cost	kosztować	kosh-**to**-vach
cot	łóżeczko	woo-**zhech**-ko
cotton	bawełna	ba-**vew**-na
cough	kaszel	**ka**-shel
counter (at post office)	okienko	o-**kyen**-ko
country	kraj	kray
country inn	karczma; zajazd	**kar**-chma; **za**-yast
credit card	karta kredytowa	**kar**-ta kre-di-**to**-va
crime	przestępstwo	pshes-**tem**-pstwo
crisps	chrupki	**hroop**-kee
crockery	naczynia kuchenne	na-**chi**-nya koo-**hen**-ne
to cross	przejść	psheyshch
cross country skiing	narty biegowe	**nar**-ti bye-**go**-ve
crossroads	skrzyżowanie	skshi-zho-**va**-nye
cruise	rejs	reys
currency	waluta	va-**loo**-ta
custom duty	cło	tswo
to cut oneself	skaleczyć się	ska-**le**-cheech she
cutlery	sztućce	**shtooch**-tse
cycling	jazda na rowerze	**yaz**-da na ro-**ve**-zhe
Czech Republic	Czechy	**che**-hi

D

damaged	uszkodzony	oo-shko-**dzo**-ni

damp wilgotny veel-**got**-ni
danger niebezpieczeństwo nye-bes-pye-**chen**-stwo
dark ciemno **chem**-no
daughter córka **tsoor**-ka
day dzień djen
dead (person) zmarły **zmar**-wi
December grudzień **groo**-djen
deck chair leżak **le**-zhak
deep głęboki gwem-**bo**-kee
delay opóźnienie o-poozh-**nye**-nye
delicious pyszny **pish**-ni
delivery dostawa do-**sta**-va
dentist dentysta den-**tis**-ta
dentures proteza pro-**te**-za
to depart (train/plane) odjeżdżać/odlatywać od-**yezh**-djach/od-la-**ti**-vach
department store dom towarowy dom to-va-**ro**-vi
departure (train/plane) odjazd/odlot **od**-yast/**od**-lot
dessert deser **de**-ser
destination cel podróży tsel pod-**roo**-zhi
detailed szczegółowy shche-goo-**wo**-vi
diabetes cukrzyca tsook-**shi**-tsa
diarrhoea rozwolnienie roz-vol-**nye**-nye
difficult trudny **troo**-dni
dinner obiad **o**-byat
direct bezpośredni bes-posh-**red**-nee
direction kierunek kye-**roo**-nek

directory książka telefoniczna **kshon**-shka te-le-fo-**neech**-na
dirty brudny **brood**-ni
disabled niepełno-sprawny nye-pe-wno-**sprav**-ni
disaster katastrofa ka-ta-**stro**-fa
discount obniżka; zniżka; rabat ob-**neesh**-ka; **zneesh**-ka; **ra**-bat
dish danie **da**-nye
divorced rozwiedziony roz-vye-**djo**-ni
doctor lekarz **le**-kash
door drzwi dzhvee
double podwójny pod-**vooy**-ni
downstairs na dole na **do**-le
dozen tuzin **too**-zheen
to do robić **ro**-beech
dress suknia/ sukienka **sook**-nya/ soo-**kyen**-ka
to drink pić peech
drinking water woda pitna **vo**-da **peet**-na
to drive a car prowadzić samochód pro-**va**-djeeech sa-**mo**-hoot
driver kierowca kye-**rof**-tsa
driving licence prawo jazdy **pra**-vo **yaz**-di
to drown utopić się oo-**to**-peech she
dry-cleaner's pralnia chemiczna/ sucha **pral**-nya he-**meech**-na/ **soo**-ha
dryer suszarka soo-**shar**-ka
dumplings pierogi pye-**ro**-gee
during podczas **pot**-chas

dustbin śmietnik **shmyet**-neek
duvet kołdra **kow**-dra

E

ear ucho **oo**-ho
early wczesny **fthes**-ni
east wschód fshoot
Easter Wielkanoc vyel-**ka**-nots
easy łatwy **wa**-tfi
to eat jeść yeshch
egg jajko **yay**-ko
electric point gniazdko **gnyas**-tko
emergency nagły wypadek **nag**-wi vi-**pa**-dek
empty pusty **poos**-ti
end koniec **ko**-nyets
engaged (the line) zajęte za-**yen**-te
engine silnik **sheel**-neek
England Anglia **an**-glya
English angielski an-**gyel**-skee
Englishman/woman Anglik/Angielka **an**-gleek/an-**gyel**-ka
enjoyable przyjemny pshi-**yem**-ni
enough dosyć **do**-sich
entrance (foot) wejście **vey**-shche
entrance (on transport) wjazd vyast
entrance fee wstęp fstemp
entry visa wiza wjazdowa **vee**-za vyaz-**do**-va
equipment sprzęt spshent

English	Polish	Pronunciation
error	pomyłka	po-**miw**-ka
escalator	ruchome schody	roo-**ho**-me **sho**-di
evening	wieczór	**vye**-choor
examination (medical)	badanie	ba-**da**-nye
excellent	doskonały	dos-ko-**na**-wi
excess baggage	nadwyżka bagażu	nad-**vish**-ka ba-**ga**-zhoo
exchange rate	kurs wymiany	koors vi-**mya**-ni
excursion	wycieczka	vi-**chech**-ka
excuse me!	przepraszam!	pshe-**pra**-sham!
exit (foot)	wyjście	**viy**-shche
exit (on transport)	wyjazd	**vi**-yast
expensive	drogi	**dro**-gee
expiry date	data ważności	**da**-ta vazh-**nosh**-chee
to explain	wyjaśnić	vi-**yash**-neech
eye	oko	**o**-ko
eye drops	krople do oczu	**kro**-ple do **o**-choo

F

English	Polish	Pronunciation
face	twarz	tfash
facilities	ułatwienia	oo-wat-**fye**-nya
to faint	zemdleć	**zem**-dlech
family	rodzina	ro-**djee**-na
fan (electric)	wiatrak	**vya**-trak
far	daleko	da-**le**-ko
farm	gospodarstwo	gos-po-**dar**-stfo
fast	szybki	**ship**-kee

father	ojciec	**oy**-chets
February	luty	**loo**-ti
to feed	nakarmić	na-**kar**-meech
to feel (well/ unwell)	czuć się (dobrze/ niedobrze)	chooch she (**dob**-zhe/ nye-**dob**-zhe)
I don't feel well	źle się czuję	zle she **choo**-ye
female	kobieta	ko-**bye**-ta
ferry	prom	prom
fever	gorączka	go-**ron**-chka
few	kilka	**keel**-ka
fiancé/fiancée	narzeczony/a	na-zhe-**cho**-ni/a
field	pole	**po**-le
to fill in (tooth)	zaplombować	za-plom-**bo**-vach
filling (tooth)	plomba	**plom**-ba
fine (OK)	dobrze	**dob**-zhe
fine (penalty)	kara	**ka**-ra
to find	znaleźć	**zna**-leshch
finger	palec	**pa**-lets
fire brigade	straż pożarna	strash po-**zhar**-na
fireman	strażak	**stra**-zhak
first	pierwszy	**pyer**-fshi
first name	imię	**ee**-mye
fish	ryba	**ri**-ba
fitting room	przymierzalnia	pshi-mye-**zhal**-nya
flat (apartment)	mieszkanie	myesh-**ka**-nye
flight	lot	lot
flood	powódź	**po**-vooch
floor (level)	piętro	**pyen**-tro
flour	mąka	**mon**-ka

flower	kwiat	kfyat
flu	grypa	**gri**-pa
fly (insect)	mucha	**moo**-ha
fog	mgła	mgwa
folk art	sztuka ludowa	**shtoo**-ka loo-**do**-va
food	jedzenie	ye-**dze**-nye
food shop	sklep spożywczy	sklep spo-**zhif**-chi
foot	stopa	**sto**-pa
football	piłka nożna	**pee**-wka **nozh**-na
footpath	ścieżka	**shchesh**-ka
for	dla	dla
for non-smokers	dla niepalących	dla nye-pa-**lon**-tsih
for smokers	dla palących	dla pa-**lon**-tsih
foreigner	cudzoziemiec	tsoo-dzo-**zhe**-myets
forest	las	las
fork	widelec	vee-**de**-lets
fortnight	dwa tygodnie	dva ti-**god**-nye
fourth	czwarty	**chfar**-ti
fracture	złamanie	zwa-**ma**-nye
free	wolny	**vo**-lni
free seat	wolne miejsce	**vol**-ne **myeys**-tse
French fries	frytki	**frit**-kee
fresh	świeży	**shfye**-zhi
Friday	piątek	**pyon**-tek
fridge	lodówka	lo-**doof**-ka
friend	przyjaciel	pshi-**ya**-chel

English	Polish	Pronunciation
frost	mróz	mroos
fruit	owoce	o-**vo**-tse
fuel	benzyna	ben-**zi**-na
full	pełny	**pe**-wni
full board	pełne utrzymanie	**pe**-wne oo-tshi-**ma**-nye
funfair	wesołe miasteczko	ve-**so**-we myas-**te**-chko
furniture	meble	**meb**-le
fuse	bezpiecznik	bes-**pyech**-neek
future	przyszłość	**pshish**-woshch

G

English	Polish	Pronunciation
game (sport)	mecz	mech
garden	ogród	**og**-root
gate (airport)	wyjście	**viy**-shche
gay (person)	gej	gey
Gents (toilet)	męska	**men**-ska
German	niemiecki	nye-**myets**-kee
German (man)	Niemiec	**nye**-myets
German (woman)	Niemka	**nyem**-ka
Germany	Niemcy	**nyem**-tsi
to get	dostać	**dos**-tach
to get lost	zgubić się	**zgoo**-beech she
to get off	wysiadać	vi-**sha**-dach
to get on (transport)	wsiadać	**fsha**-dach
to get to (on foot)	dojść	doyshch
to get to (by transport)	dojechać	do-**ye**-hach

gifts upominki oo-po-**meen**-kee
girl, girlfriend dziewczyna djef-**chi**-na
to give dać dach
glass szklanka **shklan**-ka
glasses (optical) okulary o-koo-**la**-ri
glove rękawiczka ren-ka-**veech**-ka
to go (on foot) iść eeshch
to go (by transport) jechać **ye**-hach
good dobry **dob**-ri
goodbye! do widzenia! do vee-**dze**-nya!
good morning! dzień dobry! djen **do**-bri!
good night! dobranoc! do-**bra**-nots!
grandparents dziadkowie djat-**ko**-vye
great! świetnie! **shfyet**-nye!

Great Britain Wielka Brytania **vyel**-ka bri-**ta**-nya
green zielony zhe-**lo**-ni
greengrocer's sklep warzywny sklep va-**zhiv**-ni
grocer's sklep spożywczy sklep spo-**zhif**-chi
ground floor parter **par**-ter
guesthouse pensjonat pen-**syo**-nat
guide przewodnik pshe-**vod**-neek
guided tour wycieczka z przewodnikiem vi-**chech**-ka s pshe-vod-**nee**-kyem

H

hair włosy **vlo**-si
half pół poow
half price pół ceny poow **tse**-ni
hammer młotek **mwo**-tek
hand ręka **ren**-ka
handicapped niepełno sprawny nye-pe-wno-**sprav**-ni
handicrafts wyroby artystyczne vi-ro-bi ar-tis-**tich**-ne
hangover kac kats
happy zadowolony za-do-vo-**lo**-ni
hard twardy **tfar**-di
hat czapka; kapelusz **chap**-ka; ka-**pe**-loosh
to have mieć myech
to have to; must musieć **moo**-shech
hay fever katar sienny **ka**-tar **shen**-ni
head głowa **gwo**-va
headache ból głowy bool **gwo**-vi
health zdrowie **zdro**-vye
to hear słyszeć **swi**-shech
heart serce **ser**-tse
heater grzejnik **gzhey**-neek
heating ogrzewanie og-zhe-**va**-nye
heavy ciężki **chen**-shkee
help pomoc **po**-mots
here tutaj **too**-tay
hi! (informal) cześć! cheshch!
high wysoki vi-**so**-kee

hiking wycieczki piesze vi-**chech**-kee **pye**-she
hill wzgórze **vzgoo**-zhe
hire wynająć vi-**na**-yonch
historical sights zabytki za-**bit**-kee
holiday urlop/wakacje **oor**-lop/va-**kats**-ye
home dom dom
hospital szpital **shpee**-tal
hot gorący go-**ron**-tsi
how much? ile? **ee**-le?
how often? jak często? yak **chen**-sto?
hour godzina go-**djee**-na
house, home dom dom
hunting polowanie po-lo-**va**-nye
to hurry spieszyć się **spye**-shich she
to hurt boleć **bo**-lech
husband mąż monsh

I

I'd like ...(man speaking) chciałbym **hchaw**-bim
(woman speaking) chciałabym **hchaw**-abim
ice lód loot
ice-cream lody **lo**-dee
identity card dowód osobisty **do**-voot o-so-**bees**-ti
if jeżeli ye-**zhe**-lee
ill chory **ho**-ri
in (place) w v

in the afternoon	po południu	po po-**wood**-nyoo
in the evening	wieczorem	vye-**cho**-rem
indigestion	niestrawność	nye-**strav**-noshch
injection	zastrzyk	**zas**-tshik
injured	ranny	**ran**-ni
innocent	niewinny	nye-**veen**-ni
inside	w środku	f **shrot**-koo
instead of...	zamiast...	**za**-myast...
instructions for use	instrukcja obsługi	eens-**trook**-tsya op-**swoo**-gee
insurance	ubezpieczenie	oo-bes-pye-**che**-nye
international	międzynaro-dowy	myen-dzi-na-ro-**do**-vi
to introduce oneself	przedstawić się	pshet-**sta**-veech she
to invite	zaprosić	za-**pro**-sheech
is it...?	czy to jest...?	chi to yest...?
is there...?	czy jest...?	chi yest...?

J

jacket (for man/woman)	żakiet/marynarka	**zha**-kyet/ma-ri-**nar**-ka
January	styczeń	**sti**-chen
jaw	szczęka	**shchen**-ka
job	praca	**pra**-tsa
juice	sok	sok
July	lipiec	**lee**-pyets
jumper	sweter	**sfe**-ter
June	czerwiec	**cher**-vyets

K

keep	(za)trzymać	(za-)**tshi**-mach
kettle	czajnik	**chay**-neek
key	klucz	klooch
kidney	nerka	**ner**-ka
kind (nice)	uprzejmy	oop-**shey**-mi
kitchen	kuchnia	**kooh**-nya
knife	nóż	noosh
to know	wiedzieć	**vye**-djech

L

Ladies (toilet)	damska (toaleta)	**dam**-ska to-d-**le**-ta
lake	jezioro	ye-**zho**-ro
language	język	**yen**-zik
large	duży	**doo**-zhi
larger	większy	**vyen**-kshi
last one	ostatni	os-**tat**-nee
late	późny	**poozh**-ni
later	później	**poozh**-nyey
launderette	pralnia	**pral**-nya
to leak	przeciekać	pshe-**che**-kach
leather	skóra	**skoo**-ra
to leave (on foot)	wyjść	viyshch
to leave (by transport)	wyjeżdżać	vi-**yezh**-djach
to leave (something behind)	zostawić	zos-**ta**-veech
left-luggage	przechowalnia bagażu	pshe-ho-**val**-nya ba-**ga**-zhoo
left (to turn)	lewy; na lewo	**le**-vi; na-**le**-vo

English	Polish	Pronunciation
leg	noga	**no**-ga
lemon	cytryna	tsit-**ri**-na
less	mniej	mnyey
to let (hire, rent)	wynająć	vi-**na**-yonch
letter	list	leest
lettuce	sałata	sa-**wa**-ta
to lie down	położyć się	po-**wo**-zhich she
life jacket	kamizelka ratunkowa	ka-mee-**zel**-ka ra-toon-**ko**-va
lifeboat	łódź ratunkowa	wooch ra-toon-**ko**-va
lift (elevator)	winda	**veen**-da
light (daylight)	światło	**shfyat**-wo
lighter (cigarette)	zapalniczka	za-pal-**neech**-ka
to like	lubić	**loo**-beech
lip	warga	**var**-ga
to listen to	posłuchać	pos-**woo**-hach
a little	trochę	**tro**-he
to live	mieszkać; żyć	**myesh**-kach; zhich
liver	wątroba	von-**tro**-ba
local	regionalny	re-gyo-**na**-lni
long	długi	**dwoo**-gee
to look for	szukać	**shoo**-kach
lorry	ciężarówka	chen-zha-**roof**-ka
loud	głośny	**gwosh**-ni
love	miłość	**mee**-woshch
luck	szczęście	**shchen**-shche
luggage	bagaż	**ba**-gash
luggage trolley	wózek bagażowy	**voo**-zek ba-ga-**zho**-vi

lunch	obiad	**o**-byat
lung	płuco	**pwoo**-tso

M

mail	poczta	**poch**-ta
main	główny	**gwoo**-vni
man	mężczyzna	men-**shchiz**-na
manager	kierownik	kye-**rov**-neek
many	dużo	**doo**-zho
map	mapa	**ma**-pa
March	marzec	**ma**-zhets
market	rynek; targ	**ri**-nek; targ
married man	żonaty	zho-**na**-ti
married woman	mężatka	men-**zhat**-ka
mass	msza	msha
match (game)	mecz	mech
matches	zapałki	za-**paw**-kee
mattress	materac	ma-**te**-rats
May	maj	may
may I?	czy mogę?	chi **mo**-ge?
to mean	znaczyć	**zna**-chich
measles	odra	**od**-ra
meat	mięso	**myen**-so
medication	leki	**le**-kee
medium	średni	**shred**-nee
to meet	spotkać; poznać	**spot**-kach; **poz**-nach
menu	menu; karta; jadłospis	me-**nee**; **kar**-ta; yad-**wos**-pees
message	wiadomość	vya-**do**-moshch
midday	południe	po-**wood**-nye

English	Polish	Pronunciation
midnight	północ	**poow**-nots
milk	mleko	**mle**-ko
mineral water	woda mineralna	**vo**-da mee-ne-**ra**-lna
mirror	lustro	**loo**-stro
mistake	pomyłka	po-**miw**-ka
misunderstanding	nieporozumienie	nye-po-ro-zoo-**mye**-nye
mobile (phone)	telefon komórkowy/ komórka	te-**le**-fon ko-moor-**ko**-vi/ ko-**moor**-ka
moment	chwila	**hfee**-la
monastery	klasztor	**klash**-tor
Monday	poniedziałek	po-nye-**dja**-wek
money	pieniądze	pye-**nyon**-dze
month	miesiąc	**mye**-shonts
moon	księżyc	**kshen**-zhits
morning	rano	**ra**-no
mother	matka	**ma**-tka
motorbike	motocykl	mo-**to**-tsikl
motorway	autostrada	au-to-**stra**-da
mountain	góra	**goo**-ra
mountain bike	rower górski	**ro**-ver **goor**-skee
mountain pass	przełęcz górska	**pshe**-wench **goor**-ska
mouth	usta	**oo**-sta
to move	ruszać	**roo**-shach
Mr	pan	pan
Mrs	pani	**pa**-nee
much	dużo	**doo**-zho
mug	kubek	**koo**-bek
mugging	napad	**na**-pat

mumps	świnka	**shfeen**-ka
muscles	mięśnie	**myen**-shnye
mushrooms	grzyby	**gzhi**-bi
must; **to have to**	musieć	**moo**-shech
mustard	musztarda	moosh-**ta**-rda
my (possessive) *m*	mój;	mooy;
f	moja;	**mo**-ya;
n	moje	**mo**-ye

N

name (surname)	nazwisko	naz-**vees**-ko
name (first name)	imię	**ee**-mye
napkin	serwetka	ser-**vet**-ka
nappies	pieluszki	pye-**loosh**-kee
narrow	wąski	**von**-skee
national	narodowy	na-ro-**do**-vi
nationality	narodowość	na-ro-**do**-voshch
nationality (citizenship)	obywatelstwo	o-bi-va-**tel**-stfo
nausea	mdłości	**mdwo**-shchee
near	blisko	**blees**-ko
necessary	konieczny	ko-**nyech**-ni
neck	szyja	**shi**-ya
to need	potrzebować	po-tshe-**bo**-vach
never	nigdy	**neeg**-di
newspaper	gazeta	ga-**ze**-ta
new	nowy	**no**-vi
news (TV, radio, etc.)	wiadomości	vya-do-**mosh**-chee
New Year	nowy rok	**no**-vi rok
next	następny	nas-**tem**-pni

nice	miły	**mee**-wi
nice-looking	ładny	**wad**-ni
night	noc	nots
no	nie	nye
noisy	hałaśliwy	ha-wash-**lee**-vi
nonsense	bzdura	**bzdoo**-ra
non-smoking	niepalący	nye-pa-**lon**-tsi
noon	południe	po-**wood**-nye
north	północ	**poow**-nots
Northern Ireland	Irlandia Północna	eer-**lan**-dya poow-**nots**-na
nose	nos	nos
nothing	nic	neets
November	październik	pazh-**djer**-neek
nurse	pielęgniarka	pye-leng-**nyar**-ka

O

o'clock	godzina	go-**djee**-na
occupied	zajęty	za-**yen**-ti
October	październik	pazh-**djer**-neek
of course!	oczywiście!	o-chi-**veesh**-che!
office	biuro	**byoo**-ro
off-licence	sklep monopolowy	sklep mo-no-po-**lo**-vi
often	często	**chen**-sto
oil	olej	**o**-ley
OK	w porządku; dobrze	f po-**zhon**-tkoo; **dob**-zhe
old	stary	**sta**-ri
on business	służbowo	swoozh-**bo**-vo
once	raz	ras

on foot	piechotą	pye-**ho**-tow
on the right/ on the left	na prawo/ na lewo	na **pra**-vo/ na **le**-vo
open	otwarte	ot-**far**-te
to open	otwierać	ot-**fye**-rach
opposite	naprzeciwko	nap-she-**cheef**-ko
optician	optyk	**op**-tik
or	albo	**al**-bo
orange (fruit)	pomarańcza	po-ma-**ran**-cha
to order	zamówić	za-**moo**-veech
our	nasz	nash
out of order	nie działa/ nieczynne	nye **dja**-wa/ nye **chin**-ne
outdoors	na świeżym powietrzu	na **shfye**-zhim po-**vyet**-shoo
outside	na zewnątrz	na **zev**-nonch
oven	piekarnik	pye-**kar**-neek
overland (post)	lądowa	lon-**do**-va
owner	właściciel	vwash-**chee**-chel

P

pain	ból	bool
pain killer	środek przeciwbólowy	**shro**-dek pshe-cheef-boo-**lo**-vi
palace	pałac	**pa**-wats
pancakes	naleśniki	na-lesh-**nee**-kee
pants	majtki	**may**-tkee
parcel	paczka	**pach**-ka
parents	rodzice	ro-**djee**-tse

to park	zaparkować	za-par-**ko**-vach
party	impreza	eem-**pre**-za
pasta	makaron	ma-**ka**-ron
to pay	płacić	**pwa**-cheech
payment	opłata	op-**wa**-ta
peak (mountain)	szczyt	shchit
pen	pióro	**pyoo**-ro
pensioner	emeryt	e-**me**-rit
people	ludzie	**loo**-dje
performance	przedstawienie	pshet-sta-**vye**-nye
person	osoba	o-**so**-ba
petrol	benzyna	ben-**zi**-na
pharmacy	apteka	ap-**te**-ka
to phone	zadzwonić	za-**dzvo**-neech
phonecard	karta telefoniczna	**ka**-rta te-le-fo-**neech**-na
photograph	zdjęcie	**zdyen**-che
a piece (of something)	kawałek	ka-**va**-wek
pillow	poduszka	po-**doosh**-ka
place	miejsce	**myey**-stse
plane	samolot	sa-**mo**-lot
plate	talerz	**ta**-lesh
platform	peron	**pe**-ron
play (theatre)	sztuka	**shtoo**-ka
playground	plac zabaw	plats **za**-baf
to play (instrument)	grać na...	grach na...
pleasant	przyjemny	pshi-**yem**-ni
please	proszę	**pro**-she

plug	gniazdko	**gnyas**-tko
p.m.	po południu	po po-**wood**-nyoo
pneumonia	zapalenie płuc	za-pa-**le**-nye pwoots
poison	trucizna	troo-**cheez**-na
police station	komisariat policji	ko-mee-**sa**-ryat po-**lee**-tsee
Polish	polski	**pol**-skee
Polish (man)	Polak	**po**-lak
Polish (woman)	Polka	**pol**-ka
to post	wysłać pocztą	**wis**-wach **poch**-tow
post office	poczta	**poch**-ta
postcard	kartka	**kar**-tka
poster	plakat	**pla**-kat
potato chips	frytki	**frit**-kee
potatoes	ziemniaki	zhem-**nya**-kee
pregnancy	ciąża	**chon**-zha
pregnant	w ciąży	f **chon**-zhi
prescription	recepta	re-**tsep**-ta
price	cena	**tse**-na
priest	ksiądz	kshonts
to pronounce	wymawiać	vi-**ma**-vyach
to pull	ciągnąć	**chon**-gnonch
to push	pchać	phach
pushchair	wózek	**voo**-zek

Q

queue	kolejka	ko-**ley**-ka
quickly	szybko	**ship**-ko
quiet	cichy	**chee**-hi

R

racket (tennis, etc.) rakieta ra-**kye**-ta

railway station dworzec kolejowy **dvo**-zhets ko-le-**yo**-vi

rain deszcz deshch

rape gwałt gvawt

to rape zgwałcić **zgvaw**-cheech

rash (skin) wysypka vi-**sip**-ka

to read czytać **chi**-tach

real prawdziwy prav-**djee**-vi

receipt kwit/pokwitowanie kfeet/po-kfee-to-**va**-nye

to recommend polecić po-**le**-cheech

red czerwony cher-**vo**-ni

reduction zniżka **zneesh**-ka

refrigerator lodówka lo-**doof**-ka

refund zwrot pieniędzy zvrot pye-**nyen**-dzi

to remember pamiętać pa-**myen**-tach

to rent wynająć vi-**na**-yonch

to repair naprawić; zreperować na-**pra**-veech; zre-pe-**ro**-vach

to reserve zarezerwować za-re-zer-**vo**-vach

reserved seat on train miejscówka myeys-**tsoof**-ka

restriction ograniczenie o-gra-nee-**che**-nye

retired emeryt e-**me**-rit

return ticket bilet powrotny **bee**-let pov-**rot**-ni

rib	żebro	**zhe**-bro
rice	ryż	rish
right (direction)	prawo; na prawo	**pra**-vo; na **pra**-vo
right (correct)	dobrze	**dob**-zhe
river	rzeka	**zhe**-ka
road	droga	**dro**-ga
to rob (someone)	okraść	**o**-krashch
robbery	rabunek	ra-**boo**-nek
roof	dach	dah
room	pokój	**po**-kooy
route	szlak	shlak
rubbish	śmieci	**shmye**-chee
rude	niegrzeczny	nye-**gzhech**-ni
to run (means of transport)	kursować	koor-**so**-vach
rush hour	godzina szczytu	go-**djee**-na **shchi**-too

S

safe	bezpieczny	bes-**pyech**-ni
safety	bezpieczeń-stwo	bes-pye-**chen**-stfo
to sail	żeglować	zhe-**glo**-vach
to sail from	odpływać	ot-**pwi**-vach
sailing boat	żaglówka	zha-**gloof**-ka
salad	sałatka	sa-**wat**-ka
sale	wyprzedaż	vi-**pshe**-dash
for sale	na sprzedaż	na **spshe**-dash
salt	sól	sool
salty	słony	**swo**-ni
sand	piasek	**pya**-sek

sandwich	kanapka	ka-**nap**-ka
sanitary towel	podpaska	pot-**pas**-ka
satisfied	zadowolony	za-do-vo-**lo**-ni
Saturday	sobota	so-**bo**-ta
sauce	sos	sos
sausage	kiełbasa	kyew-**ba**-sa
to say	mówić	**moo**-veech
scarf	szalik/ apaszka	**sha**-leek/ a-**pash**-ka
school	szkoła	**shko**-wa
scissors	nożyczki	no-**zhich**-kee
Scotland	Szkocja	**shko**-tsya
Scot (man)	Szkot	shkot
Scot (woman)	Szkotka	**shkot**-ka
Scottish	szkocki	**shkots**-kee
screwdriver	korkociąg	kor-**ko**-chonk

sea	morze	**mo**-zhe
seasick: *I'm seasick*	jest mi niedobrze	yest mee nye-**dob**-zhe
seat	miejsce	**myey**-stse
to see	zobaczyć	zo-**ba**-chich
see you!	do zobaczenia!	do zo-ba-**che**-nya!
self-service	samoobsługa	sa-mo-op-**swoo**-ga
to sell	sprzedawać	spshe-**da**-vach
to send	wysłać	**vis**-wach
separately	osobno	o-**sob**-no
September	wrzesień	**vzhe**-shen
to serve	podać	**po**-dach
service	obsługa	op-**swoo**-ga
serviette	serwetka	ser-**vet**-ka

English	Polish	Pronunciation
set menu	zestaw dnia	**zes**-taf dnya
shallow	płytki	**pwit**-kee
to share	dzielić	**dje**-leech
sharp	ostry	**os**-tri
to shave	golić się	**go**-leech she
she	ona	**o**-na
sheet (linen)	prześcieradło	pshe-shche-**rad**-wo
shirt	koszula	ko-**shoo**-la
shoes	buty	**boo**-ti
shop	sklep	sklep
shop assistant (male)	sprzedawca	spshe-**daf**-tsa
shop assistant (female)	sprzedawczyni	spshe-daf-**chi**-nee
shopping centre	centrum handlowe	**tsen**-troom han-**dlo**-ve
short	krótki	**kroot**-kee
shorts	szorty	**sho**-rti
shoulder	bark	bark
to show	pokazać	po-**ka**-zach
shower	prysznic	**prish**-neets
to shut	zamknąć	**zam**-knonch
to be sick	wymiotować	vi-myo-**to**-vach
sights (views to look at)	widoki	vee-**do**-kee
silk	jedwab	**yed**-vap
silver	srebro	**sreb**-ro
single (room)	jednoosobowy	ye-dno-o-so-**bo**-vi
sister	siostra	**shos**-tra

English	Polish	Pronunciation
to sit down	usiąść	**oo**-shonshch
size	rozmiar	**roz**-myar
skates	łyżwy	**wizh**-vi
to ski	jeździć na nartach	**yezh**-djeech na nar-tah
skin	skóra	**skoo**-ra
skirt	spódnica	spood-**nee**-tsa
skis	narty	**nar**-ti
sleeping bag	śpiwór	**shpee**-voor
slow	(po)wolny	(po)-**vol**-ni
small	mały	**ma**-wi
small change	drobne	**drob**-ne
smaller	mniejszy	**mnyey**-shi
to smell (nice)	ładnie pachnieć	**wad**-nye **pah**-nyech
to smoke	palić	**pa**-leech
snow	śnieg	shnyek
soap	mydło	**mid**-wo
socket	gniazdko	**gnyas**-tko
socks	skarpety	skar-**pe**-ti
soft drinks	napoje chłodzące	na-**po**-ye hwo-**dzon**-tse
some more	jeszcze trochę	**yesh**-che **tro**-he
someone	ktoś	ktosh
something	coś	tsosh
sometimes	czasami	cha-**sa**-mee
son	syn	sin
sorry!	przepraszam	pshe-**pra**-sham
sour	kwaśny	**kfash**-ni
sour milk	kwaśne mleko	**kfash**-ne **mle**-ko
south	południe	po-**wood**-nye

souvenirs	pamiątki	pa-**myon**-tkee
space	miejsce	**myey**-stse
to speak	mówić	**moo**-veech
speed	prędkość	**prent**-koshch
to spend (time/ money)	spędzać/ wydawać	**spen**-dzach/ vi-**da**-**v**ach
spicy	pikantny	pee-**kan**-tni
spoon	łyżka	**wish**-ka
spring	wiosna	**vyos**-na
stairs	schody	**sho**-di
stamps	znaczki	**znach**-kee
to start	zaczynać	za-**chi**-nach
starters	przystawki	pshis-**taf**-kee
station	dworzec	**dvo**-zhets
to steal from someone	okraść	**o**-krashch
to steal something	ukraść	**oo**-krashch
to stink	śmierdzieć	**shmyer**-djech
stomach	żołądek	zho-**won**-dek
to stop	zatrzymać się	za-**tshi**-mach she
straight on	prosto	**pros**-to
sugar	cukier	**tsoo**-kyer
sun	słońce	**swon**-tse
Sunday	niedziela	nye-**dje**-la
supper	kolacja	ko-**lats**-ya
supplement	opłata dodatkowa	op-**wa**-ta do-dat-**ko**-va
surname	nazwisko	naz-**vees**-ko
surroundings	okolica	o-ko-**lee**-tsa
sweet shop	cukiernia	tsoo-**kyer**-nya

to swim	pływać	**pwi**-vach
swimming pool	basen; pływalnia	**ba**-sen; pwi-**val**-nya
to switch off	wyłączyć	wi-**won**-chich
to switch on	włączyć	**vwon**-chich

T

table	stół	stoow
to take	zabrać	**zab**-rach
to take out (tooth)	wyrwać ząb	**vir**-vach zomp
to talk	rozmawiać	roz-**ma**-vyach
tall	wysoki	vi-**so**-kee
tap	kran	kran
taxi	taksówka	tak-**soof**-ka
taxi rank	postój taksówek	**pos**-tooy tak-**soo**-vek
tea	herbata	her-**ba**-ta
teacher	nauczyciel	na-oo-**chi**-chel
teaspoon	łyżeczka	wi-**zhech**-ka
to telephone	zadzwonić	zadz-**vo**-neech
to tell	powiedzieć	po-**vye**-djech
tent	namiot	**na**-myot
text message	es–em–es	es-**em**-es
thank you	dziękuję	djen-**koo**-ye
theft	kradzież	**kra**-djesh
there is/ there are...	jest.../są...	yest.../sow...
thick	gruby	**groo**-bi
thief	złodziej	**zwo**-djey
thin (material)	cienki	**chen**-kee

to think	myśleć	**mish**-lech
third	trzeci	**tche**-chee
thirsty (I'm)	chce mi się pić	htse mee she **peech**
this one *m*	ten;	ten;
f	ta;	ta;
n	to	to
throat	gardło	**gar**-dwo
thrombosis	skrzep	skshep
Thursday	czwartek	**chfar**-tek
ticket	bilet	**bee-let**
ticket office	kasa biletowa	**ka**-sa bee-le-**to**-va
tights	rajstopy	ray-**sto**-pi
till	kasa	**ka**-sa
till receipt	kwit; paragon	kfeet; pa-**ra**-gon
till tomorrow!	do jutra!	do **yoot**-ra!
timetable	rozkład jazdy	**ros**-kwat **yaz**-di
tin	puszka	**poosh**-ka
tin opener	otwieracz do puszek	ot-f**ye**-rach do **poo**-shek
tip	napiwek	na-**pee**-vek
tired	zmęczony	zmen-**cho**-ni
to	do	do
today	dzisiaj	**djee**-shay
toe	palec u nogi	**pa**-lets oo **no**-gee
together with	razem z...	**ra**-zem z...
toilet	toaleta	to-a-**le**-ta
tomatoes	pomidory	po-mee-**do**-ri
tomorrow	jutro	**yoo**-tro
tongue	język	**yen**-zik

tonight	dziś wieczorem	djeesh vye-**cho**-rem
tonsillitis	angina	an-**gee**-na
too expensive	za drogo	za **dro**-go
tooth	ząb	zomp
torch	latarka	la-**ta**-rka
tough (meat)	twarde	**tfar**-de
tough (difficult)	trudny	**trood**-ni
tour	wycieczka	vi-**chech**-ka
towel	ręcznik	**ren**-chneek
town; city	miasto	**myas**-to
toy	zabawka	za-**baf**-ka
traffic	ruch uliczny	rooh oo-**leech**-ni
trailer	przyczepa	pshi-**che**-pa
train	pociąg	**po**-chonk
translation	tłumaczenie	twoo-ma-**che**-nye
to travel	podróżować	pod-roo-**zho**-vach
travel agent's	biuro podróży	**byoo**-ro pod-**roo**-zhi
traveller's cheques	czeki podróżne	**che**-kee pod-**roo**-zhne
tree	drzewo	**dje**-vo
trip	wycieczka	vi-**chech**-ka
trolley	wózek	**voo**-zek
trousers	spodnie	**spod**-nye
truth	prawda	**prav**-da
to try	spróbować	sproo-**bo**-vach
to try on	przymierzyć	pshi-**mye**-zhich
Tuesday	wtorek	**fto**-rek

to turn	skręcić	**skren**-cheech
twice	dwa razy	dva **ra**-zi
tyre	opona	o-**po**-na

U

ulcer	wrzód	vzhoot
umbrella	parasolka	pa-ra-**sol**-ka
uncle	wujek	**voo**-yek
uncomfortable	niewygodny	nye-vi-**god**-ni
under	pod	pot
underground	podziemie	pod-**zhe**-mye
to understand	rozumieć	ro-**zoo**-myech
unfortunately	niestety	nyes-**te**-ti
unhappy	niezadowolony	nye-za-do-vo-**lo**-ni
United Kingdom	Zjednoczone Królestwo	zyed-no-**cho**-ne kroo-**les**-tfo
United States	Stany Zjednoczone	**sta**-ni zyed-no-**cho**-ne
unless	jeżeli nie	ye-**zhe**-lee nye
unpleasant	nieprzyjemny	nye-pshi-**yem**-ni
until	aż do	azh do
unwell	niedobrze	nye-**dob**-zhe
up	na/w górę	na/v **goo**-re
upper	górny	**goor**-ni
upstairs	na górze	na **goo**-zhe
urgent	pilny	**peel**-ni
urine	mocz	moch
to use	używać	oo-**zhi**-vach
use by...	spożyć przed...	**spo**-zhich pshet...

English	Polish	Pronunciation
useful	pożyteczny	po-zhi-**tech**-ni
useless	bezużyteczny	bez-oo-zhi-**tech**-ni

V

English	Polish	Pronunciation
vacant	wolny	**vol**-ni
vacuum cleaner	odkurzacz	ot-**koo**-zhach
vacuum flask	termos	**ter**-mos
valid	ważny	**vazh**-ni
valuable	cenny	**tsen**-ni
van	furgonetka	foor-go-**net**-ka
veal	cielęcina	che-len-**chee**-na
vegetables	jarzyny/warzywa	ya-**zhi**-ni/va-**zhi**-va
vegetarian	wegetariański	ve-ge-tar-**yan**-skee
vehicle	pojazd	**po**-yast
very/very much	bardzo	**bar**-dzo
vest	(pod)koszulka	(pot-)ko-**shool**-ka
veterinary surgeon	weterynarz	ve-te-**ri**-nash
view	widok	**vee**-dok
village	wieś	vyesh
vinegar	ocet	**o**-tset
to visit (sights)	zwiedzać	**zvye**-dzach
to visit (people)	odwiedzać	od-**vye**-dzach
visiting hours	godziny zwiedzania	go-**djee**-ni zvye-**dza**-nya

vodka	wódka	**voo**-tka
voice	głos	gwos
volleyball	siatkówka	shat-**koof**-ka
voltage	napięcie	na-**pyen**-che
to vomit	wymiotować	vi-myo-**to**-vach
to vote	głosować	gwo-**so**-vach

W

wage	wypłata	wip-**wa**-ta
waist	talia	**ta**-lya
to wait (for)	czekać (na)	**che**-kach (na)
waiter	kelner	**kel**-ner
waiting room	poczekalnia	po-che-**kal**-nya
waitress	kelnerka	kel-**ner**-ka
to walk	chodzić	**ho**-djeech
to go for a walk	iść na spacer	eeshch na **spa**-tser
walking trip	wycieczka piesza	vi-**chech**-ka **pye**-sha
wall	ściana	**shcha**-na
wallet	portfel	**por**-tfel
to want	chcieć	hchech
war	wojna	**voy**-na
warm	ciepły	**chep**-wi
to wash (clothes)	prać	prach
to wash (oneself)	myć się	mich she
washbasin	umywalka	oo-mi-**val**-ka
washing machine	pralka	**pral**-ka
washing powder	proszek do prania	**pro**-shek do **pra**-nya

English	Polish	Pronunciation
to wash up	pozmywać	poz-**mi**-vach
washing up liquid	płyn do zmywania	pwin do zmi-**va**-nya
wasp	osa	**o**-sa
watch (wrist)	zegarek	ze-**ga**-rek
to watch (tv)	oglądać	og-**lon**-dach
water	woda	**vo**-da
waterproof	nieprzemakalny	nye-pshe-ma-**kal**-ni
waterskis	narty wodne	**nar**-ti **vod**-ne
waves (sea)	fale	**fa**-le
way (route)	droga	**dro**-ga
way (method)	sposób	**spo**-soop
way in (entrance) (on foot)	wejście	**vey**-shche
way out (exit)	wyjście	**viy**-shche

English	Polish	Pronunciation
we	my	mi
weather	pogoda	po-**go**-da
what's the weather like?	jaka jest pogoda?	**ya**-ka yest po-**go**-da?
wedding	ślub	shloop
we'd like to ... please	prosimy...	pro-**shee**-mi...
Wednesday	środa	**shro**-da
week	tydzień	**ti**-djen
weekend	koniec tygodnia; weekend	**ko**-nyets ty-**god**-nya; **week**-end
weekly	tygodnik	ti-**god**-neek
weight	waga	**va**-ga
welcome! (singular/plural)	witaj!/ witajcie!	**vee**-tay/ vee-**tay**-che

well (ok) dobrze **dob**-zhe

well done (steak) dobrze wysmażony **dob**-zhe vis-ma-**zho**-ni

west zachód **za**-hoot

wet mokry **mok**-ri

wet suit kombinezon/ pianka do nurkowania kom-bee-**ne**-zon/**pyan**-ka do noor-ko-**va**-nya

what co tso

what does it mean? co to znaczy? tso to **zna**-chi?

what time is it? która godzina? **ktoo**-ra go-**djee**-na?

wheel koło **ko**-wo

wheelchair wózek inwalidzki **voo**-zek een-va-**leets**-kee

when kiedy **kye**-di

where gdzie gdje

where is/ where are...? gdzie jest/ gdzie są...? gdje yest/ gdje sow...?

where from? skąd? skont?

white biały **bya**-wi

who kto kto

wholemeal bread chleb razowy hleb ra-**zo**-vi

whose czyj chiy

why? dlaczego? dla-**che**-go?

why not? dlaczego nie? dla-**che**-go nye?

wide szeroki she-**ro**-kee

widow wdowa **vdo**-va

widower wdowiec **vdo**-vyets

wife żona **zho**-na

to win wygrać **vig**-rach
wind wiatr vyatr
window okno **ok**-no
window shop wystawa vis-**ta**-va
wine wino **vee**-no
wine bar winiarnia vee-**nyar**-nya
wine glass kieliszek kye-**lee**-shek
winter zima **zhee**-ma
with z; ze z; ze
without bez bes
woman kobieta ko-**bye**-ta
wonderful cudowny tsoo-**dov**-ni
wood (material) drewno **drev**-no
wood (trees) las las
wool wełna **vew**-na
word słowo **swo**-vo
work praca **pra**-tsa
world świat shfyat
worried niespokojny nyes-po-**koy**-ni
don't worry nie martw się **nye** martf she
worse gorszy **gor**-shi
to write pisać **pee**-sach
writer pisarz **pee**-sash
writing paper papier do pisania **pa**-pyer do pee-**sa**-nya
wrong niewłaściwy nye-vwash-**chee**-vi

X

X-ray prześwietlenie pshe-shfyet-**le**-nye

Y

yacht	jacht	yaht
yawn	ziewać	**zhe**-vach
year	rok	rok
yellow	żółty	**zhoow**-ti
yes	tak	tak
yesterday	wczoraj	**fcho**-ray
yet	jeszcze	**yesh**-che
not yet	jeszcze nie	**yesh**-che nye
you (informal, singular/plural)	ty; wy	ti; vi
you (fomal, masculine/ feminine)	pan; pani	pan; **pa**-nee
young	młody	**mwo**-di
youth	młodość	**mwo**-doshch
youth hostel	schronisko młodzieżowe	shro-**nees**-ko mwo-dje-**zho**-ve

Z

zip	zamek błyskawiczny	**za**-mek bwis-ka-**veech**-ni
zoo	zoo	**zo**-o

Polish - English

A

adidasy trainers
adwokat lawyer
aktualny up to date
alarm alarm
ale but
aleja avenue
Ameryka America
Amerykanin American (man)
Amerykanka American (woman)
amerykański American
angielski English
Anglia England
Anglik/Angielka Englishman/English woman
antyki antiques
apteka pharmacy/chemist
astma asthma
autobus bus
autobus dalekobieżny long distance bus
autobusem by bus
autokar coach
autostrada motorway

B

bać się to be afraid
bandaż bandage
bankomat cash dispenser
bardzo very
barszcz beetroot soup
basen swimming pool
basen kryty indoor swimming pool
benzyna petrol
benzyna bezołowiowa lead-free petrol
bez without
bezbolesny painless
bezpiecznik fuse
bezpieczny safe
bezpośredni direct
Białoruś Belarus
biały white
biblioteka library
biegać to run; to jog
bigos hunter's dish
bilet ticket

biodro hip
biuro podróży travel agent
biuro rzeczy znalezionych lost property office
blisko near
bluzka blouse; top
bo because
ból pain
ból głowy headache
boleć to hurt
Boże Narodzenie Christmas
brać to take
brat brother
brązowy brown
brudny dirty
Brytania Britain
brzeg rzeki river bank
brzuch stomach
budynek building
budzik alarm clock
bufet buffet
bułka bread roll
butelka bottle
buty shoes
buty górskie trekking boots
być to be
być uczulonym to be allergic
być w ciąży to be pregnant

C

cena price
centrum handlowe shopping centre
centrum miasta city centre
chciałbym I'd like to... (man speaking)
chciałabym I'd like to... (woman speaking)
chcieć to want
chleb bread
chłopak/chłopiec boy; boyfriend
choroba lokomocyjna car sickness
chory ill; sick
chwila moment
ciągnąć to pull
ciało body

ciepły warm
ciężarówka lorry
ciężki heavy
ciotka aunt
cło customs
cmentarz cemetery
co? what?
co to znaczy? what does it mean?
córka daughter
coś something
cukier sugar
cukiernia sweet shop
cukrzyca diabetes
czarny black
czasopisma magazines
Czech Czech man
Czechy Czech Republic
czek cheque
czeki podróżne traveller's cheques
czekolada chocolate
Czeska Republika Czech Republic
czeski Czech
Czeszka Czech woman
cześć! hi! (informal)
czuć się to feel
czwartek Thursday
czy jest/ czy są...? is there/ are there...?
czy można/ czy możemy ...? can I/can we...?
czy coś jeszcze? anything else?
czytać to read

D

daleko far
damska (toaleta) ladies (toilet)
danie dish
danie dnia dish of the day
data urodzenia birthday
data ważności expiry date
dentysta dentist
dla for
dla niepalących for non-smokers

dla palących for smokers
dlaczego why
do to
do jutra! till tomorrow!
do widzenia! good bye; bye-bye!
do wynajęcia to let
do zobaczenia! see you!
dobranoc! good night!
dobry good
dobry wieczór! good evening!
dobrze fine; ok
dojechać to get to (by transport)
dojść to get to (on foot)
dom house; home
dom towarowy department store
dorosły adult
doskonały! excellent!
dostać to get
dowód osobisty identity card
drewno wood
drobne small change
droga road
duży large
dworzec station
dworzec kolejowy/autobusowy railway/bus station
działać to be in working order
dziecko/dzieci child/children
dziękuję thank you
dzień dobry! good morning!
dziewczyna girl; girlfriend
dzisiaj today

E

emeryt pensioner
esemes text message

F

fabryka factory
frytki French fries

Polish - English

fryzjer damski/ męski hairdresser's (women's/ men's)
funt sterling pound sterling

G

galeria sztuki art gallery
garderoba cloakroom
gardło throat
gazeta newspaper
gdzie where
gdzie jest/ gdzie są...? where is/ where are...?
głęboki deep
głośno loudly
głowa head
gniazdko electric point/ socket
godzina hour; time
która godzina? what time is it?
godziny urzędowania office hours
godziny zwiedzania visiting hours
gorący hot
góry mountains
gospodarstwo farm
gotowany boiled
grać to play
grudzień December
grzyby mushrooms

H

hala targowa (indoor) market place
hamulce brakes
handlowe (centrum) shopping centre
herbata tea
herbatniki biscuits

I

ile how much
ile kosztuje? how much is it?
imię first name
impreza event; party
inny another one
instrukcja obsługi instruction for use

iść to go (on foot)

J

jabłka apples
jadalnia dining room
jadłospis menu
jajko egg
jak często how often
jakość quality
jarzyny/warzywa vegetables
jaskinia cave
jechać to go (by transport)
jeden one
jedzenie food
jedzenie na wynos take-away food
jelita bowels
jesień autumn
jeszcze nie not yet
jeszcze trochę some more
jeszcze raz once again
jeść to eat
jezioro lake
język tongue; language
jeździć na nartach to ski
jubiler jeweller
jutro tomorrow
już already

K

kac hangover
kantor bureau de change
karczma country inn
kark nape of the neck
karta/menu/jadłospis menu
karta kredytowa credit card
karta pokładowa boarding card
karta telefoniczna phone card
kasa cash point *or* ticket office

Polish – English

kaszel cough
katar sienny hay fever
kawałek a piece of
kawiarnia café
kąpiel bath (to have a)
kciuk thumb
kiedy when
kieliszek wine glass
kiełbasa sausage
kierownik manager
kierunek direction
kilka a few
kino cinema
kiosk kiosk
kiszka gut
klatka piersiowa chest
klimatyzacja air conditioning
klucz key
koc blanket
kolacja supper
kolano knee
kolejka linowa cable car
koło ratunkowe life belt
komisariat policji police station
komórkowy telefon (komórka) mobile (phone)
koniec end
kontrola celna customs control
korek uliczny traffic jam
kostka u nogi ankle
kostka u ręki wrist
kosztować to cost
ile to kosztuje? How much does it cost?
komisariat policji police station
koszula shirt
koszulka t-shirt
koszyk basket
kościół church
kość bone
krew blood
kręgosłup spine
krople drops (of liquid)
książka book

księgarnia bookshop
ktoś someone
która godzina? what time is it?
który? which one?
kuchnia kitchen
kupić to buy
kurczak chicken
kurs wymiany exchange rate
kursować to sail; to go; to run (means of transport)
kurtka short coat
kwas non-alcoholic fermented drink
kwaśne mleko sour milk
kwaśny sour
kwiaciarnia flower shop
kwiecień April
kwit till receipt

L

las wood
latarnia morska lighthouse
lato summer
lawina avalanche
lądowa overland
lekarz doctor
lekcja lesson
lepiej better
lewo left (direction)
leżak deck chair
lipiec July
list letter (to post)
listopad November
Litwa Lithuania
lody ice-cream
lornetka binoculars
lotnicza by air mail
lotnisko/port lotniczy airport
ludzie people
luty February

Ł

ładny nice-looking
łatwy easy
łazienka bathroom

Polish - English

łódź ratunkowa lifeboat
łowić ryby to fish
łóżko bed
łyżwy skates

M

maj May
majtki knickers; pants
mały small
makaron pasta
mapa map
marzec March
masło butter
maślanka buttermilk
matka mother
mąż husband
meble furniture
męska gents (toilet)
mężatka married woman
mgła fog
miasto town; city
mieć to have
mieszkanie flat; apartment
miejsce place
miejsce urodzenia place of birth
miejscówka reserved seat on train
mieszkać to live
międzyna-rodowy international
mięsień muscle
mięso meat
migdałki tonsils
miło poznać nice to meet you
miska bowl
mleko milk
młody young
mniejszy smaller
mój my; mine (masculine)
mokry wet
morze sea
most bridge
mówić to speak
mrożonki frozen foods
msza mass (church)
musieć to have to; must

N

na dole downstairs
na górze upstairs/up
na lewo/ na prawo to the left/ to the right
nadbagaż excess baggage
najbliższy nearest
najlepszy the best
naleśniki pancakes
należeć to belong
namiot tent
napiwek tip
napoje drinks
naprawić to repair
naprzeciwko opposite
narty skis
narty biegowe cross country skis
narty wodne waterskis
następny next
nazwisko surname
nazywać się to be called (name)
nerka kidney
nic nothing
nic do oclenia nothing to declare
nie no
nie mówię po polsku I don't speak Polish
nie rozumiem I don't understand
niedaleko not far
nie dotykać do not touch
nie działa doesn't work/ out of order
niebezpieczeństwo danger
niebieski blue
niedziela Sunday
Niemcy Germany
Niemiec German (man)
niemiecki German adj
Niemka German (woman)
niepełnosprawny disabled
niestety unfortunately
niewidomy blind (sightless)
noc night

Polish – English

noclegi accommodation
noga leg
nos nose
nowy new
nowy rok New Year
nudny boring
numer wewnętrzny extension number
nurkowanie diving

O

odbiór (bagażu) collection (of luggage)
obiad dinner
obniżka discount
obok next to
obsługa service
obuwie shoes
obywatel citizen
ocet vinegar
oczy eyes
oczywiście of course
oddychać to breathe
oddział department
odjazd departure
odjeżdżać to depart
odlot departure (flights)
odpływać to sail from
odprawa check in
odwołany cancelled
odzież clothes
oferta offer
ograniczenie limit
ogrzewanie heating
okazje bargains
okienko counter (at post office)
okno window
oko eye
okolica surrounding area
okraść to steal from someone
olej oil
oliwa olive oil/ machine oil
opłata payment/ charge
opóźnienie delay
osoba person

osobisty	personal
ostatni	last one
ostatnie wezwanie	last call
ostrożnie!	careful!
otwarte	open
otwierać	to open
owoce	fruit

P

paczka	parcel; box
padać	to fall
pada deszcz/ śnieg	it is raining/ snowing
pan/pani	Mr/Mrs/ you (formal; singular; masculine/ feminine)
palec	finger
palenie wzbronione	no smoking
palić	to smoke
paliwo	fuel
papryka	pepper (vegetable)
paragon	till receipt
parasol	umbrella
parking	car park
parking strzeżony	attended carpark
parówki	frankfurters
parter	ground floor
pchnąć	to push
pensjonat	guesthouse
peron	platform
pęcherz	bladder
pić	to drink
piechotą	on foot
pieczywo	bakery products
piekarnia	baker's
pieluszki	nappies
pieniądze	money
pieprz	pepper (spice)
pierogi	dumplings
pierś	breast
pierwszy	first one
piękny	beautiful

Polish - English

pięta heel
piętro ground floor
pilot remote control; pilot
piłka ball
pisać to write
piwnica basement/ cellar
piwo beer
placek cake
plaża beach
plecy back
plomba filling (tooth)
płuco lung
płyn liquid
pływać to swim
pływalnia swimming pool
po after
po angielsku in English
po polsku in Polish
po południu in the afternoon
pociąg train
początkujący beginner
poczekalania waiting room
poczta post office
podać to serve; to give
podbródek chin
podczas during
podróż travel; journey
podwójny double
pogoda weather
pogotowie ratunkowe ambulance
pokazać to show
pokład deck (ship)
pokój room
pole field
polowanie hunting
pół half
północ midnight
południe midday
połączenie connection
pomidor tomato
pomoc help
pomoc drogowa breakdown service
poniedziałek Monday
ponieważ because
popielniczka ashtray
posłuchać to listen to
pościel bedding

postój taksówek taxi rank
pośladek buttock
potrzebować to need
potwierdzić to confirm
powiedzieć to tell
powietrze air
powodzenia! good luck!
powrotny return (ticket)
poznać to meet
pożyczyć to lend; to borrow
później later
pracować to work
prać to wash clothes
pralka washing machine
pralnia dry cleaner's
pralnia chemiczna/sucha dry cleaner's
prawo jazdy driving licence
prędkość speed
prom ferry
prosić to ask
prosimy please/we'd like...
prosto straight on
proszek do prania washing powder
proszę please/I'd like...
proteza dentystyczna dentures
prysznic shower
przechowalnia bagażu left-luggage
przed before; in front of
przed południem a.m.
przedsta-wienie performance
przejście crossing
przejście dla pieszych pedestrian crossing
przejście podziemne underground passage
przepraszam excuse me/I'm sorry
przerwa break (interval)

Polish - English

przesiąść się to change (place/means of transport)
przestępstwo crime
przewodnik guide
przez across
przychodnia lekarska surgery
przyczepa trailer
przyjazd arrival
przyjeżdżać to arrive (train)
przykro mi! I'm sorry!
przylecieć to arrive (plane)
przylot arrival by plane
przymierzalnia fitting room
przymierzyć to try on
przynajmniej at least
przypadkowo accidentally
przystanek autobusowy bus stop
przystawka starter; side dish
pudełko box
pudełko zapałek matchbox
pusty empty
puszka tin

R

rabat discount
rachunek bill
ramię arm
ratownik lifeguard
ratusz town hall
raz; dwa razy once; twice
razem z... together with...
recepta prescription
rejs boat trip
reklamacja complaint (about a purchase)
remont closed for refurbishment
ręcznik towel
ręka hand
robić to do
Rosja Russia
rower bicycle
rozkład jazdy timetable
rozmawiać to talk
rozmiar size

rozmowa conversation
rozwiedziony divorced
rozwolnienie diarrhoea
również also
ruch uliczny traffic
ruszać się to move
ryba fish
rzeka river
rzeźnik butcher's

S

sala hall
sałata lettuce
sałatka salad
samolot aeroplane
sąd law court
schronisko młodzieżowe youth hostel
ser cheese
serce heart
sierpień August
skaleczyć się to cut oneself
skała rock
skarpety socks
skąd where from
sklep shop
skontaktować się to contact
skóra leather/skin
skręcić to turn
skrzyżowanie crossroads; junction
słodycze sweets
słońce sun
Słowacja Slovakia
słowo word
służbowo on business
sobota Saturday
sok juice
sól salt
spieszyć się to hurry
spódnica skirt
spodnie trousers
spożywczy food store
spóźnić się to be late
spróbować to try
sprzedawać to sell
sprzedawca salesman
sprzedawczyni saleswoman
sprzedaż sale

stacja benzynowa petrol station
stacja kolejowa railway station
statek ship
staw pond
staw joint (part of body)
stopa foot
straż pożarna fire brigade
strażak fireman
styczeń January
suknia/sukienka dress
surówka raw vegetable salad
suszarka dryer
Sylwester New Year's Eve
syn son
szatnia cloakroom
szczegółowy detailed
szczęśliwy happy
szewc shoe repairer
szklanka glass (drinking)
szkoła school
szlak route
szpital hospital
szukać to look for
szyja neck
szynka ham

Ś

ściana wall
ścieżka footpath
ścieżka rowerowa cycling path
śniadanie breakfast
śmieci rubbish
średni middle size
środa Wednesday
śródmieście town centre
światło light (daylight)
świeży fresh

T

tak yes
targ market place
targi fair (trade fair)
temu ago
ten/ta/to this one (*m/f/n*)
tłusty fatty (food)

torba bag
trasa route
trawa grass
trochę a little bit
tutaj here
twardy hard
twaróg soft white cheese
twarz face
ty you (singular informal)
tygodnik weekly
tylko only

U

ubezpieczenie insurance
ubranie clothes
uczulenie allergy
Ukraina Ukraine
ukraść to steal something
ulgowy with concession
ulica street
umieć to be able to
umówić się to make an appointment
upominki small gifts; souvenirs
urlop holiday
urodzić się to be born
usiąść to sit down
usługi services
usługi dla klientów customer service
usta mouth
uszkodzony damaged
uwaga attention; caution

W

waga scales; weight
wakacje holiday
waluta currency
wanna bath tub
warga lip
warsztat samochodowy garage (repairs)
warzywa/jarzyny vegetables
ważny important
wąski narrow

Polish - English

wątroba liver
wczoraj yesterday
wegetariański vegetarian
wejście entrance (on foot)
wełna wool
wesołe miasteczko fairground (funfair)
wędka fishing rod
wędliny cold meats
wewnętrzny internal
wiadro bucket
wieczór evening
wieczorem in the evening
wiadomość message
wiadomości news
Wielkanoc Easter
więcej more
większy larger
winda lift (elevator)
winiarnia wine café
wino wine
wiosna spring
witajcie! welcome! *pl*
wjazd entrance (by transport)
wliczone included (in the bill)
włamać się to break into (a building/car)
właściciel owner
włączyć to switch on
włożyć to put on
włóż monetę insert the coin
woda water
woda bieżąca running water
woda do picia (woda pitna) drinking water
woda niezdatna do picia do not drink the water
wolne miejsce free seat
wolny free; available
wódka vodka
wózek bagażowy luggage trolley
wózek inwalidzki wheelchair
wschód east
wsiadać to get on/in
wspinaczka climbing

wstęp admission
wstęp wolny admission free
wstęp wzbroniony no entry
wszystko all; everything
wszystkiego najlepszego! all the best!
wtorek Tuesday
wybielacz bleach
wyciąg krzesełkowy chair lift
wycieczka trip
wycieczka piesza walking trip
wyjazd exit (by transport)
wyjeżdżać to leave (by transport)
wyjście exit (on foot)
wyjść to leave (on foot)
wyłączyć to switch off
wymienić pieniądze to change money
wynająć to rent; to let
wypadek accident
wyprzedaż sales
wyrwać ząb to take out a tooth
wysiadać to get off
wysłać to send
wysoki tall; high
wzbronione forbidden
wzgórze hill

Z

z plecakiem backpacking
z wyżywieniem with food
za behind
za drogo too expensive
za granicą abroad
zabytki historical monuments; sights
zachować to keep (to retain)
zachód west
zaczynać (się) to start
zadowolony glad; happy
zadzwonić to ring; to telephone
zajazd country inn

Polish – English

zajęte engaged (occupied)
zamknięte closed
zamówić to order
zamykać to close
zapałki matches (box of)
zapłacić to pay
zaparkować to park
zaplombować to put in a filling (tooth)
zarezerwować to reserve
zatrzymać się to stop
zawołać to call
ząb tooth
zdążyć na... to catch... (bus; train; etc.)
zdrowy healthy
zepsuty broken
zgadzać się to agree
zgubić się to get lost
zgwałcić to rape
zimny cold
złamać to break
zły bad
zmienny changeable
znaczki stamps
znaczyć to mean
zniżka discount
zobaczyć to see; to look at
zraniony injured
zreperować to repair
zwiedzać to visit (places)
zwierzę animal
zwrot pieniędzy refund

Ź

źle not good; not well
zły bad

Ż

żebro rib
żona wife
żonaty married man
żur sour rye soup with sausage
życzyć to wish

Further titles in Collins' phrasebook range
Collins Gem Phrasebook

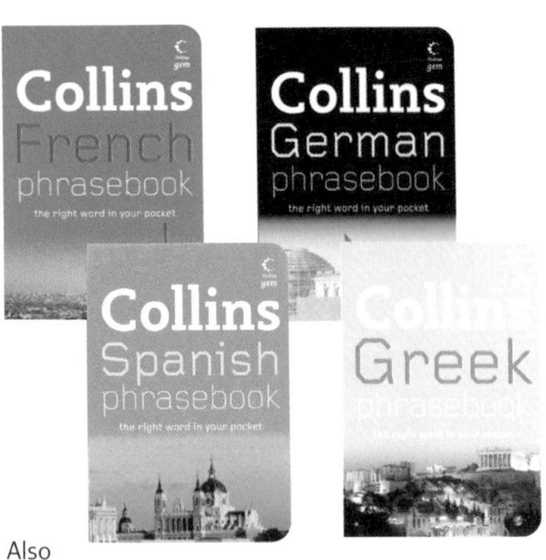

Also
available as **Phrasebook CD Pack**

Other titles in the series

Arabic	Greek	Polish
Cantonese	Italian	Portuguese
Croatian	Japanese	Russian
Czech	Korean	Spanish
Dutch	Latin American Spanish	Thai
French		Turkish
German	Mandarin	Vietnamese